ONLY PLAYING, MISS

ONLY PLAYING, MISS

*The Playscript and a Workshop Approach to the
Problem of Bullying*
Penny Casdagli and Francis Gobey
with Caroline Griffin

tb

Trentham Books
in association with the
Professional Development Association

Only Playing Miss
Play by Penny Casdagli first published in 1989 by The Neti-Neti
Theatre Company, 44 Gladsmuir Road, London N19 3JU.
Tel: 071-272 7302.

© 1990 Penny Casdagli and Francis Gobey

First published in 1990 by
Trentham Books Limited
13/14 Trent Trading Park
Botteslow Street
Stoke-on-Trent
England ST1 3LY

British Library Cataloguing in Publication Data
Casdagli, Penny
    'Only playing, Miss!': the playscript and workshops in schools
    I. Title II. Gobey, Francis III. Griffin, Caroline
    822.914

ISBN: 0-948080-40-X

Acknowledgement (p.138):
Back in the Playground Blues
by Adrian Mitchell
(from M. Rosen. Kingfisher Press, 1985)

Cover image by Ingrid Pollard.

Typeset by The Design Bureau, Wrexham
and printed in Great Britain by BPCC Wheatons Ltd, Exeter

Contents

PREFACE

David Lane of the Professional Development Foundation,London.

The Neti-Neti Theatre Company has produced a powerful drama about bullying. It exposes the complex web of relationships which surround the experience. As a piece of theatre it works exceptionally well. Their series of supporting workshops enables schools to begin to understand the problem and take action. Pupils, parents and teachers can begin to talk to each other and break the conspiracy of silence that often accompanies the issue of bullying.

The Professional Development Foundation became aware of the work of Neti-Neti early in the development of the play *Only Playing, Miss*. We encouraged them to write this book so that their ideas could be made widely available. This preface considers the value and particular strengths of their work in the context of approaches to dealing with bullying.

What is bullying?

Bullying is one of those hidden subjects. We all know it goes on and would certainly take action when confronted with it but there have been few attempts to find out how much misery is being caused by bullying in school every day.

The publication of the first book in the United Kingdom devoted to the issue, *Bullying In Schools* (Trentham Books 1989) reviewed the available statistics. According to Delwyn Tattum, bullying may involve 870,000 children. This would make them the largest pupil group who have special needs in England and Wales.

Many tragic cases have been reported in the press over the years. There are examples of pupils with disabilities being terrorised, children being driven to suicide and even cases of murder. Many children have been forced out of the system altogether and into truancy.

The first problem with bullying concerns the definition of the act. Heinemann, (1973) originally reported on an activity he called 'mobbing', referring to a group attack on an individual who had disturbed the group's ordinary activity. Later work has referred to both individual and group action (Olweus, 1978). The inclusion of psychological or physical threat in definitions of bullying also raises problems since there are 'established' sex differences for these types of bullying (Roland 1988).

The intention of the aggressor and the belief of the victim are considered key aspects by some researchers (Stephenson and Smith, 1988. Lane,1988) and therefore school reports cannot be relied upon to reflect the situation accurately . Unfortunately, teachers often seriously underestimate the level of the problem in their own schools.

The definition of the term is of more than academic interest, for it has led to different perspectives on intervention. Pikas (1989), for example, has concentrated on a concept of mobbing closer to Heinemann's original definition. He has developed very effective techniques for working with mobbers and victims. Olweus and Roland (1983) and Roland (1988) have taken a different route and developed anti-bullying campaigns for use in schools. It is unfortunate that these have sometimes been seen as opposing alternatives rather than the ends of a dimension of potential approaches. This confusion over terms has led to difficulties in determining the level of such activities.

What is apparent is that the way the problem is viewed by those involved is of critical importance. The play *Only Playing, Miss* shows these different points of view very neatly. The experience of the writer/director in developing the play, and the workshops, led by the Education Officer, add to this framework. They identify the difficulties that the subject can create, as old memories are stirred and old guilt and shame re-experienced.

We asked Neti-Neti to write about the experience of the play, not just provide a commentary on the text. Bullying is not a topic to be introduced and then dropped to make space for the next topic. It touches the lives of those involved very intimately and deeply.

How much bullying takes place?

The answer depends on how the theoretical perspectives are viewed. Are we to separate group violence, calling that 'mobbing', from individual violence, calling that 'bullying' — or are we to view them as part of one set of social aggression in which a dominant individual or group intends and causes distress to another? It is this later perspective which has influenced UK work and which is used in various forms in the UK incidence studies.

Establishing the level, type and duration of bullying has not proved easy even in the well-financed research studies in Scandinavia. Figures reported there vary between 5% and 25%.

Some welcome clarity was offered in the UK by an important study from Stephenson and Smith (1988). Based on research with over 1,000 primary aged children, they estimate that 23% of children experience bullying. Bullying is not a passing phase, they point out. For many children, the pain continues over years.

The figures are shocking but they conceal the pain and humiliation felt by those involved. The characters in *Only Playing, Miss* bring that pain to life. It can be seen, heard and felt, and also tackled.

Who, then, might be at risk? It could be anyone. The following examples quoted in Tattum and Lane, (1989) illustrate this. Chazan, based in Infant Schools in South Wales, has described both individual bullies and bullying gangs of six and seven year olds. Herbert, a Head of Year at a Huddersfield High School, has referred to the incidents of intimidation, extortion, physical threats, the destruction of homework, and psychological bullying. He argues that it is not only physical violence that children fear but also the constant condemnation, isolation and loneliness. Askew, from her research in London schoools, has reported on clever children who have just given up, and children constantly feeling that they have to be careful in case they become the next victim. She makes the key point that it is not just the victim who suffers but also all the children who have to keep their heads down, just in case. Walford, although describing the long history of gross violence in public schools as days of Flashman that may have passed, still calls for vigilance. For, as he points out, for the victim in the boarding school, unlike day school pupils, there is no escape from the tormentors.

These patterns describe pupil-to-pupil activity, but Lane (1988) has pointed to the social-psychology of a process which labels children as bullies but not their teachers. The pupils in his research identified about 10% of teachers as bullies. Conversely, there are teachers who felt bullied by children (Sparks, 1983). Bullying is a more complex process than is implied by popular stereotypes of bullies and victims.

What are the causes of bullying?

If in fact bullying is a complex social labelling process, then understanding its causes requires more than looking at bullies and victims.

Roland (1988) has argued that bullying is more likely to be a group than an individual activity and that it must be seen as part of the social process of group activity. Bullying among boys is more likely to be part of power-based social relationships; for girls, affiliation activities are more frequently the source of bullying activities. Both bullies and victims are likely to have fewer close friends than average. Physical characteristics are a factor, particularly differences in physical appearance and strength, but the importance of these are generally overestimated. Any feature could be picked on as a pretext for bullying. Low self-esteem seems to be a common feature of victims and some come to see themselves as deserving of their fate. For Roland, the socialisation process is a key feature. Olweus refers to 'personality' factors and the role of early learning, particularly a tolerance of aggressive behaviour.

Chazan (1988) also points to the combination of a difficult temperament and adverse parental attitudes and practices. Stephenson and Smith (1988) point to a relationship between social deprivation and bullying (for bullies and victims). They also identify groups of bullies and victims who vary on a number of personality, physical and social dimensions. Their data raises the key issue of different possible interventions for these groups. However, they also argue for the presence of key differences between schools. There are schools with high and schools with low incidences of bullying. The distinctions between these schools are not just of catchment area and intake, but of policy decisions by the schools. The school's own role in promoting or reducing bullying therefore becomes an important consideration.

The nature of the relationships between the participants is often complex and interdependent. The bully does not exist without the victim. Understanding that interplay, sometimes subtle, sometimes gross, is important in developing policies for tackling bullying. The text provided by Neti-Neti sensitively explores that relationship in the case of one group of children.

Some schools show ambivalence in attitudes to power and masculinity. A violent macho ethos may be promoted by staff as well as pupils, whereby, bullying becomes a status activity. A failure to deal with these issues clouds attempts by a school to state a clear policy on equal opportunities. If, for example, women teachers in a school feel intimidated by the tactics of some male staff towards them and feel that they will not get a fair hearing, how safe will children feel in reporting incidents of bullying?

Askew(1988), has clearly demonstrated the role played by these issues, in her research into boys' schools. She has also provided evidence that action, even by one form teacher, can have positive effects.

What can be done?

Twenty-five per cent of teachers asked claimed that is is sometimes helpful to ignore the problem but the majority of children look to teachers to act (Stephenson and Smith, 1988). Given the misery that many thousands of children endure for several years of their lives, and the fact that the school is itself part of the problem, schools cannot afford to take an ostrich-like position on bullying. The concept of 'safe school' which has begun to take hold in the USA is perhaps one that should be explored here (Lane, 1989).

So, can anything be done? Herbert (1988) has demonstrated that it can. Using the academic and pastoral curriculum, he has helped both victims and bullies to change the way they behave.

Numerous individual programmes by teachers working with individuals and groups, initiating curriculum approaches and policy changes, have recently been emerging and resource suggestions are available (Titman,1988, Lane,1989). Internationally, a variety of ideas have emerged and these show both the breadth of concern and the range of methods adopted in different countries (Roland and Munthe, 1989).

Neti-Neti provides another way of approaching this problem. The use of drama is very powerful. It touches the feelings, it is involving and it provides a mechanism for exploring situations. It is an innovative way into this complex problem.

A comparison of the recommendations by Pikas (1975) and more recently suggestions by Tattum (1988), indicates the emerging trend. Both highlight the need for awareness of the problem and for careful work with bullies (or mobbers) and victims. Tattum points, however, to the greater emphasis on the victim in the USA, while in the UK, there is stress on the involvement of parents, community responsibility and the role of the academic and pastoral curriculum. In fact, a whole school policy is beginning to emerge.

One theme is, perhaps, shared by all those working in this field. Children, parents and teachers are entitled to live without fear in their schools. It is for the school to take action, to establish a whole school policy which creates an environment in which all feel valued and safe.

A workshop approach through drama.

Before children can raise the issue of bullying, they have to feel safe. The conspiracy of silence has to be broken. How are we to get children and teachers talking about the problem?

The playscript and workshops in this book are a powerful tool for developing the necessary awareness which is a precondition for action. Together with their forthcoming video and the live performances by the Neti-Neti Theatre Company of *Only Playing, Miss*, the book offers schools a way to share ideas between children and teachers.

I have seen the play, talked to teachers who have used it, and watched the effect on children. I have no doubt of its value as part of a co-ordinated approach to bullying. I am pleased to include it alongside the Foundation's other publications in this area and strongly recommend it.

Our pupils deserve careful, tried and effective approaches to the problem of bullying. They have suffered in silence too long.

AN INTRODUCTION TO
'ONLY PLAYING, MISS'

Only Playing, Miss is a play about bullying. Its unashamed objective is to stop bullying. Within its limits, it depicts the behaviour of most of the common protagonists in the bullying scenario: 'victim','bully', observer, the one who tells, the group, the teachers and adults and, most importantly, the friend. By exposing this extraordinarily complex and painful phenomenon, it tries to understand why bullying takes place and, while offering no easy solutions, suggests some ways of dealing effectively with bullying that might be considered both by young people themselves and by their carers. It is also only a piece of theatre. Yet all of us involved in the project believe (and have only had that belief strengthened by seeing the play in action) that theatre can cause change, and that a piece of work reflecting this belief can also be a moving and satisfying theatrical experience. Indeed, if *Only Playing, Miss* had failed as a play, it wouldn't have mattered how 'worthy' the intention behind it was. Without stirring thoughts and feelings, it would simply have been a piece of didactic exposition.

From the first, the response to *Only Playing, Miss* was extremely positive: long lists of schools waiting to book it, many more than we could accommodate; attention from the media; the letters and writings sent to us from our audiences. This showed that a play about bullying was long overdue and much wanted. But this was not why *Only Playing, Miss* was undertaken. The idea was suggested by a child and by her experience.

One day I went to collect a friend, aged eight, from school — something I don't often do. Just within the school gates, a group of children had surrounded a small boy crouching under a thin urban tree. They were shouting advice to him, or shouting at him, yet none of them broke through that circle to touch him or try to make him do some of the things he was being told. I was struck by his gaze fixed on the ground immediately before him, and by his body poised ready to run, yet motionless. I looked to my friend for an explanation. She clearly knew the sort of thing that was going on — it was 'child-only' — and she dragged me away. 'He's probably been hit.' I saw his sister come from outside. Still he was transfixed. I went and found a teacher and told him what I had seen. He quickly went out to the playground, the circle scattered and I saw him hug the child, who was trembling.

Some time later, my friend began to be bullied. She told the adults that care for her. They listened carefully and were naturally very upset. They alerted the school immediately. But bullying was in the air, and the conditions in which it thrives were all present. Many of the children lived in very stressful situations and had needs that could not be met by the school alone. There was a high turn-over among the teachers, the ones remaining becoming more and more demoralised. It wasn't only my friend that was being bullied. Other children were suffering. One young teacher was being bullied by her class. And my friend, with great honesty, told us she was sometimes bullying younger children.

My friend's mother and carers went to the school several times, saw the Head Teacher, and gave any help they could. But the situation seemed to have slipped out of everyone's hands. My friend walked out of school on more than one occasion and wasn't missed until she arrived at home. She began to school-refuse. She was often ill. The school said there was nothing more they could do. It was Christmas 1988.

In January 1988, I was due to work with Second Year of acting students at the Guildhall School of Music and Drama, where I had often worked before, devising and directing the 'Schools Tour'. The brief was fairly open: a piece of about an hour's duration was to be worked on with the students' active participation. It was then to play in up to ten schools in one week. The project was designed to give the students first hand experience of working for young audiences and an opportunity to contribute to a devising process. The rehearsal time allowed was twenty two hours' rehearsal a week for five weeks, including the devising, writing and teaching process. Although it was a risk, as time was short, I determined to make no plans or preparations before meeting the students. We would start at the same point and whatever we did would be as much a discovery for me as it would for them. There was only one word that I was going to take in with me and that was 'bullying'. We would do something about bullying and perform it in my friend's school. It was the only helpful contribution I could think of to make. Nothing else I had done seemed very effective.

The group of twelve students, predominantly white, represented half the year. As the year had been randomly divided by the staff, the students had no choice over which group they worked in nor did they know in advance what the subject of my project was. When I said 'we are going to do something about bullying' there was a short silence and then immediately we started to work, for that word 'bullying' had elicited a strong response.

The first part of rehearsals was devoted to an examination of the subject. We shared experiences as well as doing private writing. Neti-Neti's Co-Artistic Director, Caroline Griffin had given me some worksheets on bullying and two short television plays which consider the same bullying incident from the victim's and the bully's point of view respectively. We watched the plays and did the worksheets. Our research material was very limited but during those first weeks, *Bullying In Schools* edited by Delwyn Tattum and David Lane appeared. It was the first major book devoted to bullying to be published in the British Isles and was extremely useful to us.

One of the responsibilities of a director of young people's work is to evolve a close knowledge of audiences, and an acute awareness of what is appropriate for various ages. I had initially intended our piece to be for top Juniors — I wanted it to play in my friend's school. However, it soon became clear that the material our particular group was generating was for an older age group. We took a decision at the end of the first week of rehearsals to play for first and second year secondary students (eleven to thirteen year olds) — in other words, for one of the most difficult audiences there is.

As a climate of trust and interest developed within the group, more first-hand experiences were volunteered, including accounts of serious and prolonged acts of physical and psychological abuse. As I have mentioned, these students were not specially chosen for this project. This showed us all how commonplace and painful bullying is. The membrane of protective memory had broken. We were freshly shocked by violence, both our own and that of others, and wanted to understand more. We started to analyse and devise.

We had to deduce the general from the specifics of our own experience. Several powerful improvisations were recorded on tape and transcribed. There were many points we wanted to make, and some characters that had emerged. Caroline Griffin, herself also a teacher, came to rehearsals to advise us about school procedures and to help us with the role of Mrs. Richards, the teacher. At the end of the second week, I took all that we had gathered and started constructing a story-line and writing dialogue.

As the story took shape, so the devising and writing technique developed. I would identify a gap in the narrative or a point we needed to make and set up a specific improvisation. Everyone had a turn at more or less every part. A tape recorder was used to record the dialogue while the Stage Manager wrote down the moves of the improvisation as they happened. The improvisations were then transcribed by myself and a devoted stage management team. I used these as a basis for the dialogue of the play, sometimes verbatim, but more frequently edited and juxtaposed differently. The group soon became very skilful and able to cover large areas of the story in a short space of time. I was very conscious that as this was part of a students' training course, each of the twelve students had to have a proper part to play. This made the play long, at one hour and ten minutes.

The play was completed by the Wednesday evening of the final week of rehearsals. This left two sessions for the play to be rehearsed, the casting having been settled some days before. Music and songs were added on the final Saturday morning before we opened on the Monday.

The opening performance was played in a so-called 'tough' secondary school in the ILEA area that had not had any theatre group visiting it for four years. The students, performing for the first time in their training to the 'public', did an excellent show. The two hundred-strong audience were quickly engaged and spontaneously cheered Mrs. Richards when she told off the bullies, Rant and Cheesey. They clapped loudly at the end. As often happens, the 'toughest' audiences are often the most responsive.

The students completed their tour of ten schools in one week most success-fully. Because we were so struck by the audiences' keen response to the play and the teachers' enthusiasm, Caroline Griffin and I decided that funding should be secured for Neti-Neti to present a professional multi-lingual production of the play in the Autumn of that year.

We knew from our researches that there was little documentation of young people's and adults' responses to bullying in their own words. We therefore approached the Sir John Cass's Foundation for funding to make possible the post of an Education Officer to Neti-Neti. We also asked the Foundation for help to publish a programme containing the playscript together with a selection of young people's writing that we hoped would result from the writing work-shops to be led by the Education Officer. We also knew that Trentham Books were extremely interested in publishing a book on the *Only Playing, Miss* project. This was encouraging. While most of the actual text has been written by Francis and myself, the author's credit reflects the valuable work, both structural and editorial, put in by Caroline.

Thames Television had approached the Company some months before about making a documentary on our work. It did not happen but we were offered the option of making a *Help!* programme instead. We now took Thames up on this offer. Two *Help!* programmes were made using extracts of *Only Playing, Miss* as a catalyst for discussing the problem of bullying. Thames provided an excellent free fact sheet, prepared in consultation with Michele Elliott of Kidscape, for any viewer who wanted it. In the programmes, Neti-Neti asked for viewers to write to us with their experiences of bullying to help us prepare for the Autumn production. We also asked the permission to quote from the letters, as we wanted to publish adult experience alongside young people's writing in order to point to the long-term effects of bullying.

The Company received over forty letters. We read them with a great feeling of respect for the writers, and often we wept. Those letters were our touchstone. I kept them by me through all the re-writing and revisions of the play. The actors read them in rehearsal as did the journalist Norma Cohen, who quoted from them in her excellent article on the play for the *Times Educational Supplement.* Extracts from the Thames letters appear in a later section of this book, together with some extracts of letters written to the Young Guardian on the same subject. The Neti-Neti production of *Only Playing, Miss,* like most of our previous work, was to be performed multilingually in English, Sign Language and Bengali. Becky and Mrs. Richards were to be played by deaf actresses. There are an increasing number of highly professional deaf performers. However, at that time not more than five members of Equity out of a membership of over 44,000 were, to our knowledge, Bengali-speaking. Two were men, and the remaining three actresses were not available. We therefore outreached Shanaz Choudhury, who interrupted her studies to come and join us, to play the part of Hashi. We persuaded Equity to give us an extra union card to make this possible.

All the cast had to be or become fluent in Sign Language and did so under the excellent supervision of Paula Garfield, our Signing Advisor. Jobaidur Rahman translated passages of the text into Bengali and tutored us in that language.

Working multilingually is an enriching experience, and we believe it to be an implicitly anti-racist act. Many of our audiences are seeing their mother tongue used on stage for the first time. By placing minority languages next to each other, as with Sign Language and Bengali, the status of each language is raised, as the dominance of English is creatively challenged. This also helps to dispel the commonly held misapprehension that British Sign Language (BSL) is a gestural substitute for English. BSL is a language in its own right, reflecting the particular culture of the world from which it arises.

We work in Bengali specifically to serve schools with a high population of Bengali-speaking pupils, such as those in the Borough of Westminster and in Tower Hamlets. One future development for Neti-Neti is that both management and performers will learn more Bengali and it will be used more widely by all characters in our plays whenever possible.

Working for deaf and hearing audiences and for audiences that have English as a second language demands writing conceived with respect to different perceptions right from the start. Great visual clarity, firmness of purpose, attention to focus as well as a frame of easily communicated reference points are all qualities needed to inform the work. *Only Playing, Miss* presents the world of school which is familiar to all children. The function of the patches of narration are for certain characters to establish a relationship with the audience, to set the scenes and to emphasise any changes in time and place.

Only Playing, Miss is mainly performed in Sign Supported English (SSE) which is not, in fact, a language at all. It follows the syntax and word order of spoken English not that of BSL. It uses signs to amplify the meaning of the verbal language and is enormously expressive and effective as a means of communication.

BSL is used particularly by Mrs. Richards when she describes Eugene's suffering, and by Becky in her direct address to the audience. The world of *Only Playing, Miss* assumes a totally integrated school situation in which all pupils and teachers are fluent in Sign and some Bengali as well as English. The two scenes that take place outside school in Eugene's home and in Rant's are interpreted in BSL while the characters talk in English. This seemed realistic and also gave us an opportunity to explore the possibilities of interpretation which we had never made part of stage action before. The actresses playing Becky and Mrs. Richards stood on chairs behind the action to interpret. Although this was entirely functional, their presence contributed a great deal theatrically by intensifying attention and by adding a feeling that the problems in both homes were being witnessed and understood. For the rest of the play, all the performers signed and spoke simultaneously.

Ideas on how to use the Playscript, Video and Workshop Exercises

The workshop exercises are conceived as discrete from the play and can be used in any situation that seems most appropriate — for example, to open out the experience of bullying and strategies to deal with the phenomenon in Tutor Group time, as part of a Personal and Social Education programme, or in English or Drama curriculum time.

Similarly, the playscript can be read before or after the Workshop Exercises. The characters in *Only Playing, Miss* show many of the familiar responses of 'bully', 'victim', 'bystander', 'teacher' and 'friend' and reading the play can take pressure off students from revealing too much about themselves on a sensitive issue while still being able to discuss the issue itself.

Both the playscript* and the video** of *Only Playing, Miss* lend themselves to 'prediction' exercises — stopping at particular points and discussing what will happen next and why and for re-working the ending by the students themselves.

That the playscript and the video make their points in several languages should encourage the many forms of communication in our multi-lingual, deaf and hearing classooms to take the floor also — for bullying is a passionate subject and the language of our deepest feelings is whatever we find appropriate to explore those feelings in — in classrooms, school hall, School Council meetings or wherever the responses to this play, video and workshop exercises are to be shared.

available from the Company.
** *available from Trentham Books (£39.95)*

Acknowledgements

NETI-NETI is a Zen Buddhist term meaning 'not this, not that', suggesting an idea of perfect harmony. Founded in 1987, the Neti-Neti Theatre Company expresses this idea by being fully integrated in both performers and management and by producing innovative and exciting work both for children and for adults with an emphasis on exploring not only language and communication but also the experience and perceptions of disability, particularly hidden disabilities. The Company has performed in theatres and in a variety of venues including schools, libraries, London Zoo and the British Museum.

Penny Casdagli was born in Greece and has worked extensively as an actress, writer and director for over twenty years. In 1987 she won the British Theatre Award with Drama Magazine for The Best Young People's Theatre.

Caroline Griffin was born in the Midlands in 1950. She teaches in a boys' comprehensive school in South London. Her new collection of poems *Passion is everywhere appropriate* is published by Only Women Press.

Jobaidur Rahman is well known not only as an actor but also as a writer and translator. He often works for the Neti-Neti Theatre Company, particularly in their tri-lingual Storytelling Events.

Francis Gobey was born in 1959. He has taught English, Drama, and ESL/EFL in Africa and Europe, and is now a freelance writer in London.

A workshop version of *Only Playing, Miss* was first performed by students from the Guildhall School of Music and Drama in February 1989. Penny Casdagli would like to thank Tilly Blackwood, Claire Garrigan, Adi Topol, Alana West, Naveen Andrews, John Clarke, Andrew Cryer, Ben Greenwood, Michael Kemp, Mateo Pedolo, and Peter Wingfield and especially Virginia Snyders for making the opportunity possible.

Everyone concerned with this project has been enormously supported and informed by the moving contributions of all the young people and adults who wrote to us in response to the Thames *Help!* programmes. We wish to thank each one of them and also Gerry Lyseight and Alison Townsend for the care with which the programmes were made. We would also like to thank Chris

Terrill of the BBC and his team who filmed a workshop, a rehearsal and a performance for the *Forty Minutes* documentary on bullying broadcast on 30 November 1989 on BBC 2 at 9.30 pm.

The production received financial support from the Arts Council of Great Britain; Greater London Arts; West Midlands Arts Association; Hereford and Worcester Educational Authority; Newham Educational Authority; Westminster City Council; Bucks Arts; Hammersmith and Fulham Borough Council; Shape at Eastern Arts; Thames Television, John Lewis plc and others. We are enormously indebted to the Sir John Cass's Foundation for funding Francis Gobey in the post of Education Officer and to all the students who have helped us learn more about ourselves and the kind of world we would like to live in.

ONLY PLAYING, MISS:
THE PLAYSCRIPT

Only Playing, Miss by Penny Casdagli was first performed on 31st October 1989 by:

Eugene Hickey	Neville Hutton
David Rant	Darren Lawrence
Mark Cheeseman	Jonathan Magnanti
Mr. Wallace	Jonathan Magnanti
Rant's Father	Jonathan Magnanti
Jo	Dietrich Griffiths
Mrs. Richards	Caroline Parker
Becky	Charlotte Moulton-Thomas
Hashi	Shanaz Chowdhury
Sam	Angela Sims
Mrs. Hickey	Angela Sims

Directed by	Penny Casdagli
Musical Director	Peter Nicholas
Signer Advisor	Paula Garfield
Bengali Advisor	Jobaidur Rahman
Company Manager	Rick Tame
Additional lyrics by	Caroline Griffin
Additional music by	Peter Nicholas
Co-Artistic Director	Caroline Griffin
Administrator	Karen Smith
Administrative Advisor	Gwyneth Lamb
Education Officer	Francis Gobey
Workshop Assistance	Noel McDermott

Note on the text

British Sign Language, English and Bengali, form the three languages used in this play although the majority of the text is in Sign Supported English, which is not a language in its own right.

Where British Sign Language is used THE TEXT IS WRITTEN LIKE THIS. Where English alone is used the text *is written like this*. Words expressed in Finger Spelling are W.R.I.T.T.E.N. L.I.K.E. T.H.I.S. Where the text is not in Bengali, Sign Supported English is used. Translations of Bengali and British Sign Language text are [written in brackets and like this.]

Introduction

A school hall, even a theatre — bare, except for a heap of chairs, piled up high like a bonfire. The actors have sets their props on the floor and are talking quietly with each other. The Stage Manager gives them the signal to start. Someone picks up a guitar and another a mouth organ, perhaps. Three young people step forward: the performers that are playing HASHI, BECKY and JO. They address the audience.

HASHI: হ্যালো, যে নাটকটি তোমরা আজকে দুপুর বেলা দেখবে তার নাম "অনলি প্লেইং মিস্"

[Hallo. The play you are going to see this afternoon is called 'Only Playing, Miss.']

BECKY: HALLO. PLAY THIS AFTERNOON NAME 'ONLY PLAYING, MISS.'

JO: Hallo. The play you are going to see this afternoon is called 'Only Playing, Miss.'

HASHI: এই নাটকটি বাংলা, সাংকেতিক ভাষা এবং ইংরেজীতে অভিনীত হবে।

[It will be performed in Bengali, Sign Language and English.]

BECKY: PERFORMED THREE LANGUAGES: B.E.N.G.A.L.I, SIGN LANGUAGE, ENGLISH.

JO: It will be performed in Bengali, Sign Language and English.

ALL: (*In their respective languages*) Thank you.

ধন্যবাদ

(The rest of the actors walk down to join them. They sing.)

CHEESEY: Who's going to be the victim
In our games when we punch and kick and yell?

JO: Who's going to be the one to suffer, scream and yell?

27

EVERYONE: এখন শুধু খেলছি
             এখন শুধু খেলছি
             এখন শুধু খেলছি
             [Only playing, now
             Only playing, now.
             Only playing, now.]

RANT: Who's going to be the one we bully on the playground today?

BECKY: Who's going to be the victim in the funny games we play?

EVERYONE: Only playing, now
             Only playing, now
             Only playing, now.

EUGENE: It always happens on concrete playgrounds,

HASHI: There's always someone living a life in fear.

MRS. RICHARDS: There's always got to be a scapegoat,

SAM: There's a million victims out there.

EVERYONE: Only playing, now
             Only playing, now
             Only playing, now.

             (The actors make whoops of playground noise as they grab the chairs from the pile and form them into two straight lines either side of the acting area.)

SCENE 1: THE DANGER OF THE PLAYGROUND

	SAM, HASHI and BECKY are playing leap-frog. JO cartwheels across.
JO:	Hashi!
HASHI:	Hi!
	(JO runs off)
BECKY:	STRAIGHT LINE YOU. [Get into a straight line you.]
HASHI:	You're not in a line.
SAM:	I am.
BECKY:	Bend over. MORE SPACE. CAN'T JUMP ME. IMPOSSIBLE. [I need more space. I can't jump. It's impossible.]
SAM:	O poor Becky! Difficult, isn't it?
BECKY:	It's not actually!
	(With much screaming, BECKY leaps over them.)
SAM:	O you're heavy. You'd better go on a diet.
BECKY:	STYLE ME. REAL STYLE. [I've got style. Real style.]
HASHI:	Come on, Sam.
BECKY:	FASTER.
HASHI:	Sam, get in line.
BECKY:	I like watching you upside down.
SAM:	*Here we go.*
	(As she is about to leap, she sees EUGENE who always carries a a plastic bag) *Eugene!*
HASHI:	Hi.
SAM:	Where have you been Eugene?
BECKY:	Are you all right?
HASHI:	*Come and talk to us.*
BECKY:	Come on.
SAM:	YEAH.
EUGENE:	*No.*

29

SAM:	What's the matter?
EUGENE:	I don't want to.
	(They try and get him to join in)
BECKY:	Come on.
EUGENE:	Get off, get off.
	(They make him bend over. As he does so, a piece of paper sticks out of his pocket)
SAM:	*Eugene, what's in your pocket?*
HASHI:	What's that?
EUGENE:	None of your business.
BECKY:	Go on, show us.
SAM:	*Empty your pockets.*
EUGENE:	It's just a letter.
	(They snatch it from him)
HASHI:	Is it a love letter?
SAM:	O it's a love letter!
EUGENE:	No, it isn't Sam.
SAM:	O give me a cuddle.
EUGENE:	It's not fair.
	(He tries to get it from them)
	Stop it. No, look, stop it. Give it to me. Give me my letter back.
SAM:	Read it out.
EUGENE:	*No!*
SAM:	It's all right. Read it out.
	(She snatches it from BECKY)
EUGENE:	Give me my letter.
	(As she is about to read it out, MRS RICHARDS appears)
MRS. RICHARDS:	What are you doing, Sam?
	(SAM gives it to HASHI)
SAM:	We're only playing, Miss. It's a playground, isn't it, Miss?
BECKY:	We're allowed to play in the playground, aren't we miss?

30

MRS RICHARDS:	Good to see you back, Eugene.
EUGENE:	*Yes, Miss.*
	(As soon as she is out of sight, they go back to the paper)
BECKY:	It isn't a letter at all. It's a poem.
SAM:	O Eugene! You little liar!
	(She reads it out)
SAM:	'Father' 'Why did you have to go away? Why did you have to die Leaving me alone to cry?'
EUGENE:	Give it to me. You've no right!
	(He tries to snatch it back but she continues reading it)
	'I feel lost and alone Don't know what to do except I think of you.'
	O, can I keep it Eugene?
EUGENE:	*No you can't. Give it back.*
	(MR WALLACE enters)
MR WALLACE:	*Form Two, you're making too much noise.* Miss Dowling, I can hear your voice over in the gymnasium. What's going on?
SAM:	Nothing.
MR WALLACE:	What's that in your hand, Miss Dowling?
SAM:	O nothing, sir.
	(She passes it to BECKY)
BECKY:	It's Eugene's poem.
MR WALLACE:	*Is this a poem, Hickey?* You're writing poetry now? Go to your class, girls.
	(SAM, HASHI and BECKY leave)
	Hickey, you missed my class this morning. Do you want to spend dinner time in the gym?
EUGENE:	No, sir.

MR WALLACE: Then get on your way, Hickey. Poetry! That's girls' stuff.

(EUGENE exits, watches by MR. WALLACE who then goes off in the opposite direction.)

SCENE 2: THE CORRIDOR

SAM and HASHI enter, the others behind them, and address the audience.

SAM: Our school's big.

HASHI: আমাদের স্কুল মস্তবড়
[Our school's big.]

SAM: You've got to look out for yourself.

HASHI: নিজের ভালো নিজেকেই দেখতে হবে। অন্য কেউ দেখবে না।
[You've got to look out for yourself. No one else will.]

SAM: No one else will. And look out for characters like David Rant. If you know what's good for you.

HASHI: হাঁ, সেটাই ভালো সবচেয়ে।
[Yes. It's better that way.]

SAM: Rant doesn't like anyone.

HASHI: কেবলমাত্র---
[Except...]

SAM: Except...

HASHI: মাঝেমাঝে দেখেছি ওকে বেকের সাথে কথা বলতে
[I've sometimes seen him talking to Beck.]

SAM: Yeah. So have I.

(JO, CHEESEY, RANT, and EUGENE come on. The corridor is full of students and noise. BECKY still has EUGENE'S poem.)

RANT: *Hi, Beck*

(She doesn't hear him amid the hubbub. RANT goes and taps her on the shoulder)

Becky!

BECKY: *Hallo, David.*

RANT: What's the next lesson?

BECKY: English.

RANT: I'm not going to hang around for it. I'm doing a bunk to the grave-yard.

BECKY: WHY?

RANT:	I can't stand that new teacher.
BECKY:	Mrs. Richards?
RANT:	I can't stand the grief she gives me.
BECKY:	YOU TROUBLE. [You'll get into trouble.]
RANT:	Trouble's my middle name.
BECKY:	WHAT?
RANT:	Don't you start.
BECKY:	It was nice when you came round at the week-end. My Mum really liked you.
RANT:	Yeah.
BECKY:	How is your Mum? I'd like to meet her.
RANT:	Yeah. Maybe. She's really busy. What's that? Have you written me a love letter?
BECKY:	*No. This isn't mine. It's Eugene's.* You can look at it if you like.
RANT:	Eugene? Is he back?
BECKY:	Yes. It's a poem.
RANT:	Let's see it.
	(The bell goes.)
BECKY:	Are you coming to English?
RANT:	No way.
	(He snatches the paper off her.)
	I'll improve myself by reading this. Ta ta. Oi, Cheesey, look at this!
	(RANT runs after CHEESEY. Everyone goes to class.)

SCENE 3: THE ENGLISH LESSON.

MRS RICHARDS, the English teacher, is talking to the students who sit facing her in a circle. SAM has a magazine in her hand. JO and HASHI whisper across the classroom to each other.

JO: Mr. Wallace told me he's got something for us. For the car.

HASHI: কি জিনিষ?
[What is it?]

JO: আমি জানিনা
[I don't know.]

MRS RICHARDS: Jo, Hashi, will you two be quiet.

SAM: Sorry. I can't find my pen, Miss.

MRS RICHARDS: You don't need it now, just listen. All right, we're going to go around in a circle and do a word association. Have any of you done it before?

JO: Is that like football association?

(General laughter)

MRS RICHARDS: Quiet. I say a word and you say a word that links with it. For instance, if I say 'up' you could say -

SAM: Down.

MRS RICHARDS: Exactly, Sam. We'll go round in a circle starting with you Sam. The first word — Sam stop it -

(SAM is looking through her bag)

the first word is 'father.'

SAM: Sorry, Miss...

(She waves her hand in the air)
... but I haven't got a pen. Can I borrow a pen?

CHEESEY: It's mine though.

SAM: Have you got a pen, Hashi?

HASHI: It's not mine, it's his.

EUGENE: Have you got another one?

BECKY: (To Eugene) You can use mine.

SAM:	(Sarcastically) Thanks, Becky.
MRS RICHARDS:	Stop it now. You don't need a pen now.
SAM:	I wasn't doing anything.
	(Behind MRS. RICHARDS back, thinking she can't see, she signs:)
	STUPID ANYWAY. [It's all stupid anyway.]
	(MRS RICHARDS does see)
MRS RICHARDS:	If you don't like the lesson you can leave.
	(Again, thinking she won't see, Sam gets out of her chair. Laughter)
	Go to Mr. Wallace's room.
	(She hands her a red card)
	Take this card with you.
SAM:	I was just sitting here.
MRS RICHARDS.	Go.
SAM:	I didn't do anything.
MRS RICHARDS:	Go to Mr. Wallace. Now. Hurry up.
SAM:	(As she is leaving) I don't believe this — this has never happened to me before.
	(She leaves the class reluctantly amid much noise.)
MRS RICHARDS:	Right.
	(The class calms down)
	'Father'.
EUGENE:	Mother.
BECKY:	Brother.
	(Silence)
MRS RICHARDS:	Any word that reminds you of 'brother'.
JO:	Ghostbusters!
BECKY:	WHAT?
JO:	(Acting it out) GHOST BUSTERS!
BECKY:	Oh!

MRS RICHARDS:	Wait your turn, Jo. Cheesey?
CHEESEY:	Sister.
HASHI:	Big. My big sister.
MRS RICHARDS:	That's fine, go on.
JO:	Beetle zoom-tube!.
MRS RICHARDS:	What was the last word?
CHEESEY:	That doesn't make sense: 'sister Beetle zoom-tube'.
MRS RICHARDS:	Start again, Jo, with a new word. And we'll got round in the opposite direction.
JO:	Ambulance.
MRS RICHARDS:	Fine.
HASHI:	Dead.
EUGENE:	Why are we doing this, Miss? I don't get.
MRS RICHARDS:	To show you you've got lots of words and pictures in your head and the next step is to believe that you can put them on paper and write something from yourselves that really means something to you.
CHEESEY:	Eugene writes poems, Miss.
MRS RICHARDS:	Let him speak for himself.
EUGENE:	I don't.
CHEESEY:	Liar!
EUGENE:	I don't like poetry. (To CHEESEY) Greasy hair.
MRS RICHARDS:	Settle down.
EUGENE:	Well, he has got greasy hair.
MRS RICHARDS:	Be quiet, Eugene.
EUGENE:	I don't write poetry.
CHEESEY:	(Taunting him) Ooo Eugene.
	(EUGENE tries to hit out at CHEESEY. MRS RICHARDS holds him)
MRS RICHARDS:	That's enough.
	(The bell rings for the end of class)
	The rest of you go. Eugene, you stay behind.

EUGENE: (To CHEESEY) Greasy.

BECKY: I liked your poem anyway, Eugene.

MRS. RICHARDS: Now all of you go.

                    (The rest of the class leave)

                    Now. Eugene, why did you behave like that?

EUGENE: Cos I felt like it, that's why.

MRS. RICHARD: What's going on?

EUGENE: None of your business.

MRS. RICHARDS: Look, I heard about your father. And I'm very, very sorry.
                    It must have been such a sad Christmas, but you can't
                    come into school and hit out at people.

EUGENE: No.

MRS. RICHARDS: It's not going to happen again, right?

EUGENE: I get angry.

MRS. RICHARDS: Of course you do. I understand that. Look, if you come in
                    in the morning and you're feeling sad or angry or whatever
                    it is, let me know. Come and see me and we'll see if we
                    can sort it out. Okay? Fair? Is that fair, Eugene?

EUGENE: Yeah.

MRS. RICHARDS: Okay. Off you go then. I'll see you tomorrow.

                    (MRS. RICHARDS leaves. EUGENE steps forwards and
                    sings this song:)

                    EUGENE'S SONG
                    There's a fire in my chest
                    That no one can see.
                    There's a fire in my head
                    And it's burning me.
                    If you say you're sorry
                    The fire's supposed to go,
                    But you don't get near me,
                    The fire keeps saying 'NO.'

                    Don't tell me it's fair,
                    Don't tell me to calm down.
                    You want me to forget

তোমরা চাও আমি ভুলে যাই
[You want me to forget.]

If I set the school on fire
It couldn't burn hotter than me,
And all the paper burning
Couldn't burn faster than me.

There's a fire in my chest.
A fire in my head.
Don't tell me it's fair.
Don't tell me to forget.

(speaking) Don't tell me to forget my Dad....

SCENE 4: THE CAR SEAT

HASHI and JO step forward and address the audience.

HASHI: যত শীগ্গির আমরা পেরেছি
[As soon as we could —]

JO: As soon as school was over, we went to see Mr. Wallace.

HASHI: তোমরা ভাবতেই পারবে না উনি কি দিয়েছেন আমাদেরকে – আমরা তৈরী করেছি তার জন্যে। যে গাড়ীটা
[You'll never guess what he gave us ——for the car we're building.]

(They run off and come back with a car seat, singing 'Go, greased lightning!')

JO: It just needs straightening out and it'll fit.

HASHI: It's brilliant.

JO: It needs stitching.

HASHI: We could easily find another one.

JO: What do you think happens when you die?

HASHI: When we die? I think we go up in the sky and wait and wait until we've forgotten our own names and then get re-born again.

JO: I can't imagine my Dad dying.

(He looks down at the car seat. There is a pause)

HASHI: I know.
এটাতো ড্রাইভারের সিট, তাই না?
[This is the driver's seat, right?]

JO: হ্যা, নিশ্চই।
[Yes, definitely.]

(RANT enters)

RANT: All right, Jo, Hashi? What have you got?

JO: Look at this! It's for the car we're building.

HASHI: This is going to be the driver's seat.

JO: It's virtually ideal. It just needs straightening out, right.

HASHI: It needs sewing.

RANT: My mum could do that. No problem.

JO:	Would she?
RANT:	Could, could, I said. No, she's too busy for that. Are we still going to Brighton when the car's finished?
JO:	হ্যাঁ, নিশ্চই।
	[Yes definitely.]
	(RANT sits in the car seat and starts singing)
RANT:	'We're going down to Brighton,oh oh! We're going down to Brighton, oh oh!'
JO:	(anxiously) That's the driver's seat, Dave. You want to be in the back. I'll be driving.
	(RANT is suddenly threatening)
RANT:	You'll only be driving if I say so. Got it?
HASHI:	You missed a brilliant English lesson David.
RANT:	Why?
HASHI:	Sam got sent out.
JO:	Eugene started freaking out.
RANT:	What did Cheesey do?
HASHI:	Eugene tried to hit him.
RANT:	What!
JO:	It's true.
RANT:	What happened?
JO:	He had to stay behind.
RANT:	Is that all? It's all right for Eugene, innit. He can do what he wants. Everyone's dad dies sooner or later.
HASHI:	Where were you?
RANT:	Keep your nose of my business. No, Eugene is seriously out of order.
JO:	He's taking his problems out on his mates.
RANT:	He needs some discipline. And if the teachers won't do it... I've got to find Cheesey anyway. See ya!
HASHI:	Yeah.
JO:	Bye.

HASHI: এটা ও পাচ্ছে না। এটা ড্রাইভারের সিট্। তুমি চালাবে গাড়ী। এবং
              আমাকে সামনে বসতেই হবে।
              [He's not having this. This is the driver's seat. You're
              driving. And I've got to be in front.]

JO: Yeah, because you're doing the navigating.

HASHI: হাঁ, নিশ্চই
              [Yes, definitely.]

SCENE 5: AT THE BUS STOP.

Sam and Becky are waiting at the bus stop.

SAM: Where's that bus?

BECKY: COLD. IF ME RUN HOME THERE NOW. [If I'd have run home, I'd be there by now.]

SAM: Stop moaning.

BECKY: YOU SHOULD HAVE S.L.U.M.B.E.R. PARTY BIRTHDAY.

SAM: *A slumber party for my birthday.* That's a good idea.

(MRS RICHARDS enters with a bag)

BECKY: GOODNIGHT.

MRS RICHARDS: Goodnight, girls.

(BECKY waves and exits)

SAM: *Oh, Mrs. Richards. Mrs. Richards!*

(She runs after her and taps her on the shoulder)

I like your sweater.

MRS RICHARDS: Thank you, Sam.

SAM: It must have been lovely when it was new. Mrs Richards?

MRS RICHARDS: *Yes?*

SAM: Can I show you something? Look.

(She gets out a pencil and holds it up)

This is the pencil I couldn't find so you sent me to Mr. Wallace. It's funny, isn't it, it doesn't look that important but it got me into a whole lot of trouble.

MRS RICHARDS: I didn't send you out because of a pencil, as you well know.

SAM: Cheesey told me Eugene Hickey was verbally abusive and violent in your lesson and hit Cheesey and called him greasy. He didn't get no punishment. It's not fair.

MRS RICHARDS: Why do you think that was, Sam?

SAM: I don't know, Miss, I can't see into teachers' minds.

43

MRS RICHARDS: Don't be ridiculous, Sam. You've got someone who looks after you, haven't you?

SAM: Yeah. So what?

MRS. RICHARDS: And I expect you love them?

SAM: Course I do! I think the world of my Mum and Dad. What are you trying to say?

MRS. RICHARDS: And if one of your parents or any of your family or friends died suddenly, you'd be very upset, wouldn't you?

SAM: That's got nothing to do with it.

MRS. RICHARDS: You're a clever girl, Sam. Think about it: the difference between losing a pencil and losing someone you love. Think how you'd feel. Wouldn't you be angry? Wouldn't you be sad?

SAM: It's not the same. You picked on me for nothing.

MRS. RICHARDS: You were disturbing the class.

SAM: Was it only me though, was it?

MRS. RICHARDS: GOODNIGHT.

SAM: (calling after her) It's not fair.

SCENE 6: THE PLAYGROUND

JO and HASHI step forward.

JO: Nothing much happened that morning.
ঘটেছে নাকি?
[Did it?]

HASHI: না [No]

JO: Except, at dinner time, in that most dangerous of places...

HASHI: সেই সাংঘাতিক জায়গায়
[In that most dangerous of places —]

BOTH: THE PLAYGROUND.

(There is a whoop of playground noise, and everyone comes out to play. EUGENE walks quietly on his own. SAM runs up to him)

SAM: Cheer up, Euge. Want to play?

(Before he can answer, she grabs his plastic bag)

Oi, Cheesey, catch!

(She throws it to Cheesey. Cheesey throws it back to SAM who throws it to RANT. EUGENE desperately tries to get it back. They freeze as each one says their thoughts.)

RANT: You used to be our mate, prat.

BECKY: HATE THIS GAME. [I hate this game.]

SAM: I'm glad it's not me.

CHEESEY: Eugene called me greasy.

JO: Eugene's okay, and so is his poetry.

HASHI: নিজের জন্যে রুখে দাঁড়াও, ইউজিন
[Stand up for yourself, Eugene.]

(RANT breaks the freeze by throwing the bag back in SAM'S direction. She deliberately lets it fall and its contents scatter. EUGENE goes to pick up his things. RANT hits him on the side of the head and as he does so, says:)

RANT: Little Euge. You know what I heard yesterday, Eugene mate?

EUGENE:	Leave me alone.
RANT:	The girls caught you with a poem! Little Euge!
	(He hits him on the side of the head again and laughs. Some of the others join in.)
EUGENE:	Leave me alone.
RANT:	This is serious. Stop laughing, Euge. Eugene!
	(RANT hits him)
	I think it's time for a trial.
EUGENE:	*Leave me alone.*
RANT:	*Steady. Cheesey.*
	(He indicates CHEESEY to hold EUGENE down.)
	Hear ye, hear ye. There is going to be a court case.
EUGENE:	Why?
RANT:	Because I don't like your face, right. Members of the Special Patrol Group, bring Eugene Hickey to the Court please!
	(SAM screams with laughter. CHEESEY salutes)
CHEESEY:	*Yes sir.*
SAM:	Chop his nose off!
EUGENE:	You're so childish.
	(He tries to make a break for it. RANT and CHEESEY pull him back viciously. As SAM goes to kick him, and they start to drag him away, with the others looking on, there is a freeze. MRS RICHARDS gets up and walks to the group but talks to the audience. JO and HASHI follow and speak the English translation over the British Sign Language.)
MRS RICHARDS:	THEN R.A.N.T. GANG TOOK HIM CHANGING ROOMS AND HAVE TRIAL PRETEND. THEY SAY EUGENE GUILTY. BAD BEHAVE AND POETRY WRITING. THEY BAD HIM NAMES. HE SHAMED. HIM PUNISHED. RANT NAMED QUOTE S.U.P.E.R. U.S.U.A.L. QUOTE. THEY HIT BRUISE SPIT ON HIM. BUS MONEY STOLE. SHINS KICKED. LEAVE HIM IN SHOWERS.

JO: And then Rant and some of his gang took him away to the changing rooms where they held a mock trial.

HASHI: Eugene was found guilty of anti-social behaviour and writing poetry. They humiliated him by calling him names. His punishment was what Rant called 'The S.U.P.E.R. U.S.U.A.L.' Eugene was beaten, bruised, and spat on. Then they stole his bus fare, kicked him in the shins, and left him in the showers.

MRS RICHARDS: But I didn't suspect any of this at the time. And nor did his mother:

SCENE 7: EUGENE'S FLAT.

MRS HICKEY is sitting on a chair, sewing buttons on a shirt. It is night. EUGENE enters. This scene is interpreted in sign by BECKY and MRS. RICHARDS sitting at either side of the acting area.

MRS HICKEY:	*What are you doing up?*
EUGENE:	*I couldn't sleep, Mum. I was hot. I was just going to get some water.*
MRS HICKEY:	*I'll go and get you it.*
EUGENE:	*No, it's alright.*
MRS HICKEY:	*What's this you've got there Eugene?*

(She is looking at his shoulder and arm)

EUGENE:	*It's nothing.*
MRS HICKEY:	*You've bruised yourself Eugene.*
EUGENE:	*Yeah, I was playing indoor cricket. I went into the nets.*
MRS HICKEY:	*It's worse than that. Look at your hand.*
EUGENE:	*It was a cricket ball.*
MRS HICKEY:	*You must tell me when you hurt yourself. You can't go round looking like that. Are you sure you're all right?*
EUGENE:	*Yeah.*

(MRS HICKEY touches his arm)

MRS HICKEY:	*All right?*
EUGENE:	*Yeah.*
MRS HICKEY:	*Now go off to bed.*
EUGENE:	*What are you doing, Mum?*
MRS HICKEY:	*I'm mending your father's shirt. I know it's daft but I miss him and it needed doing. Now off to bed. You've got to be up early for school tomorrow. I'll get the water.*
EUGENE:	*I don't think I feel well, Mum.*
MRS HICKEY:	*You'll be all right in the morning.*

(They each go their different ways. The whole Company comes on to sing the following song:)

SONG

I've given up trying to say my name.
My name has just become a game.
They kick it around and laugh at what they've found.
If I show that I care, they copy me and stare.
তাই আমি শিখেছি শব্দটি না করতে
আমার মুখ যখন মাটিতে ঠেসে ধরা তখনও।
[So I've learnt not to make a sound.
Even when my face is pushed in the ground.]
I'm trying not to show any pain.
Hoping that will spoil the fun of the game.

I'm never picked for football unless they want to kick me.
Never hear a joke unless the joke's about me.
They laugh at how I eat.
They trip me in the street.
There's always something new.
জানিনা কি করব আমি।
[I don't know what to do...]

But I've learned not to make a sound
Even when my face is pushed in the ground.
I'm trying to hold back my pain.
আমি আর স্কুলে যেতে চাই না কখনও।
[And I never want to go to school again.]
And I never want to go to school again.

SCENE 8: PASS THE BOGEY.

The changing-rooms. RANT is singing and kicking a can around. CHEESEY is also there. So is JO. He is tying his shoe.

RANT: (Singing) 'If only I could, I'd make this world a better place...'

(JO looks at them. He very deliberately finishes tying his laces, and with his foot, throws his bag up into the air, and then catches it. He looks directly at RANT as he too sings:)

JO: (Singing) 'Don't ask me what I think of you, you might not get the answer that you wanted to.'

(JO exits)

RANT: What's his problem? Have you got that quid you owe me, man?

CHEESEY: What quid?

RANT: Don't tell me you've forgotten?

(He grabs CHEESEY'S arm and twists it up his back)

CHEESEY: Yeah, I got it.

(RANT lets him go and CHEESEY gives him a pound. RANT pockets it and then sings and kicks a crisp packet around)

RANT: Give you a game.

CHEESEY: Are we gonna eat those crisps or what?

(EUGENE enters with his plastic bag and crosses to his locker)

RANT: Ah, Little Euge!

(He hits him on the side of the head. EUGENE says nothing.)

Ooooo Eugene's in a mood.

(He mocks him)

Oh no, oh no, Eugene don't touch me, Eugene the hard man. Eugene leave me alone. I'm not hard enough. Eugene please!

(He suddenly changes his tone)

	All right, mate? Good. You're looking good, Eugene, isn't he Cheesey?
CHEESEY:	You're looking so good.
RANT:	Come on. I know how to cheer you up. We'll play your favorite game. (Nicely) Sit down. (Nastily) Sit down.

(He forces EUGENE down into a chair)

And you've got the centre chair again. Little Euge.

(He hits the side of his head)

How does he manage it? I've heard all the girls are after you. Isn't that true, Cheesey?

| CHEESEY: | Yeah. |
| RANT: | No wonder. Hey lad, who's this? Who's this? |

(He imitates EUGENE)

'I'm a poet but I don't know it.' Eugene the Bard!

(They both laugh)

Come on, it's time to play....

(He conducts CHEESEY to join in)

| BOTH: | Pass the Bogey. |

(They indicate an old training shoe is the 'bogey'. RANT throws it to CHEESEY, CHEESEY to RANT, RANT to EUGENE who drops it)

| RANT: | Oh Eugene. |
| CHEESEY: | Oh, you've dropped it. |

(They beat EUGENE up)

| RANT: | Round Two. |

(CHEESEY throws it to EUGENE. He catches it, EUGENE throws it to RANT who deliberately drops it)

RANT:	Oh Eugene, don't hit me. Oh no, Eugene, don't hit me.
CHEESEY:	Go on, get him, Eugene. Get him, get him.
RANT:	Didn't we see your Dad yesterday, on Oxford Street wasn't it? It was him, wasn't it, Cheesey?

(CHEESEY catches on)

CHEESEY:	I thought he looked familiar.
RANT:	What did you do last weekend? Did he cook you a good Sunday lunch?
	(He throws the shoe at EUGENE)
CHEESEY:	Oh Eugene.
RANT:	You've dropped it again.
CHEESEY:	Oh Eugene.
RANT:	You silly, silly boy. I didn't want to have to do this to you. But we're going to have to.
	(They beat him up again.)
EUGENE:	*Let me alone... alone.*
RANT:	Okay, okay. Keep cool.
	(They stop hurting him)
	Bye then, Eugene and oh yes — give my love to your father.
	(He blows him a mock kiss)
	See you tomorrow. Same time. Same place.
	(They leave. EUGENE cries. JO enters. He pauses and stares at EUGENE.)
JO:	Eugene?
EUGENE:	*Leave me alone!*
	(JO runs out of the changing room and circles the stage. He finds MR WALLACE. He goes up to him.)
JO:	Sir?
MR WALLACE:	Johnson?
JO:	Sir, I think you'd better see Eugene. He's crying again.
MR WALLACE:	What lesson have you got Johnson?
JO:	History, sir.
MR WALLACE:	You'll be late.
	(JO exits. MR WALLACE goes to EUGENE who is still crying.)

Right, Hickey, what's the matter with you, eh? Come on, stand up lad. Eugene Hickey, stand up. Come on. Come on. Is that your bag, Hickey? Come on lad, pull yourself together. How am I supposed to help you if you won't tell me what's the matter, Hickey? Is it about your father? We heard about it and we're sorry but if you spent more time in your games lesson then you wouldn't get into trouble. Is it the boys in the Fifth Year, eh? Grow up, lad. It's a tough world out there, boy. Now pull yourself together. What lesson are you supposed to be in?

EUGENE: History.

MR. WALLACE: What?

EUGENE: History.

MR. WALLACE: Well get your things and get off there or you'll get in trouble there as well. You want to start taking part a bit more, Hickey. Pull yourself together, stand up straight, come on.

EUGENE: I do take part.

MR. WALLACE: Come on then. Are you all right now? Take your bag and get off to your lesson. I'll tell Mr. Armstrong you're going to be a bit late.

(MR. WALLACE exits. EUGENE kicks his bag and then the chair he has been sitting on and exits in the opposite direction, still crying.)

SCENE 9: CHEESEY TAKES A TUMBLE

HASHI steps forward with an old and battered fog lamp.

HASHI: The next day I was walking through the park. I'd found a fog lamp for the car and I was taking it home to mend.

(HASHI stops to try to unscrew the glass. CHEESEY enters.)

CHEESEY: Hashi! Love of my life!

HASHI: Cheesey!

(She looks at him)

What's the matter?

CHEESEY: Nothing, right. Get off my back, will you?

HASHI: Where's David?

CHEESEY: How should I know? Where's Jo?

HASHI: Why?

CHEESEY: Is that for the car?

HASHI: Yeah.

(As she looks at it again CHEESEY suddenly breaks into song:)

CHEESEY: Oh, I'm sitting in the park
Waiting for you-oo-oo!

(HASHI takes no notice, still trying to unscrew the glass on the lamp as she starts to walk off)

It's broken.

HASHI: It isn't. It's stuck.

CHEESEY: Did you nick it?

HASHI: No, I did not!

CHEESEY: Come on, give it here. I'll do it for you.

HASHI: No, it's okay.

CHEESEY: Let's have a look.

(He tries to grab it)

HASHI: I can do it myself, thanks.

CHEESEY: I said I'll do it.

HASHI: You don't know how.

CHEESEY: It's stupid that car is. It's a dream. That car won't get you
            to Brighton. It won't even get you to the nearest rubbish
            dump!

HASHI: So what? It's what we want to do, right?

CHEESEY: Is it?

            (He pushes her again.)

            Look at me when I'm talking to you.

            (She looks at him)

HASHI: Okay, I'm looking. Now what?

CHEESEY: Don't push me, Hashi, or you'll make me very cross.

HASHI: Leave it out, Mark. You'll be sorry if you don't.

CHEESEY: Oh, I will, will I? Hashi. Love of my life -

            (He goes towards her again arms outreached. She bends
            down and puts the fog lamp on the ground out of harm's
            way, catches one of his arms and throws him over her
            shoulder and to the ground.)

HASHI: Don't say I didn't warn you.

            (CHEESEY for a moment is gob-smacked, then he picks
            himself up and quickly runs off.)

SCENE 10: THE SLUMBER PARTY

BECKY and HASHI step forward.

HASHI: শনিবার, স্যামের জন্মদিন ছিল। আমরা সবাই গিয়েছিলাম ওর বাসায়।
[Saturday was Sam's birthday. We were round at her house.]

BECKY: SATURDAY SAM'S BIRTHDAY. WE HER HOUSE. [Saturday was Sam's birthday. We were round at her house.]

(SAM stands on a chair singing and signing and doing her Kylie Minogue impersonation: 'I should be so lucky...')

BECKY: Great, Sam.

(BECKY waves her hands in the air as some deaf people do instead of clapping and HASHI claps)

HASHI: Your turn, Becky.

(SAM jumps off the chair)

SAM: Truth, dare or double-dare? Chose.

BECKY: All right.

SAM: Hurry up!

BECKY: Truth.

SAM: Turn round.

(BECKY does)

I know what to ask her.

(BECKY looks over her shoulder)

Turn round. You're cheating.

(BECKY turns away again.)

SAM: TEASE HER. SAY HER BOYFRIEND E.U.G.E.N.E.! [Let's tease her. Let's say Eugene is her boyfriend.]

HASHI: BUT SHE LIKE D.A.V.I.D. [But she likes David.]

SAM: ME KNOW THAT STUPID. [I know that, Stupid.]

(She goes over and taps BECKY'S shoulder)

Ready. Becky, is it the truth that you really really like Eugene?

(HASHI giggles)

HASHI: Come on.

(SAM is giggling too)

SAM: But do you?

BECKY: A proper question, come on.

HASHI: Do you really like Eugene?

BECKY: I don't like anyone at the moment.

HASHI: I thought you liked David Rant?

BECKY: Well, I don't.

SAM: But do you really really like Eugene?

(Pause)

SAM: Come on.

BECKY: Yes, I do.

(SAM screams with laughter)

SAM: I don't believe it.

BECKY: What's wrong with Eugene?

SAM: He gets special treatment. And his poetry's rubbish.

(She laughs)

BECKY: Stop it.

(SAM continues laughing)

SAM: Ah, Becky, Becky.

BECKY: You're so childish.

SAM: We're childish! How dare you. It's my birthday!

BECKY: You know what he's been through?

SAM: So?

BECKY: He's nice to you and you're so horrible to him.

(SAM laughs with disbelief)

SAM: *Nice!* Oh Becky, Becky, tell us what you like about him best. Is it his poetry? Or his clothes? Or the way he cries?

BECKY: He's a nice boy. Better than all the rest of you.

SAM: What do you mean?

HASHI:	Stop it, you two. It's only a game.
BECKY:	He's never hurt anyone's feelings and that more than I can say for you.
SAM:	Whoa! That's quite an achievement!
BECKY:	Exactly.
SAM:	If you want to be a member of this gang, you can't like Eugene, can she Hashi?
BECKY:	Who are you to tell people what to do and who to like?
HASHI:	Don't go on any more.
SAM:	Would you like to be with Eugene now?
BECKY:	Yes, I would.
SAM:	Then I'll tell you something. Eugene's father isn't really dead. He's run off.
BECKY:	Who said?
SAM:	Wouldn't you like to know, nosey!
BECKY:	I don't believe it.
SAM:	Are you calling me a liar?
BECKY:	Yes I am.
SAM:	(Chanting) Becky loves Eugene, Becky loves Eugene.
	(BECKY pushes a chair over and runs out)
SAM:	I'm going to tell my Mum. Honestly. And it's my birthday!

SCENE 11: THE MEAL.

HASHI and JO step forward.

JO: David Rant often talked about his Mum. But I'd only ever seen him with his father.

HASHI: Me too.

(Behind them, RANT sits at the dinner table. HASHI and JO leave. MR. RANT enters with a plate of steak. This scene is sign interpreted, MR. RANT by MRS. RICHARDS and BECKY for RANT)

MR RANT: *Isn't it done enough?*

RANT: *It's red.*

MR RANT: *It's a treat.*

(RANT pokes at it with his fork)

I'll take it back. I'll cook it some more.

RANT: *Don't bother.*

(He puts tomato sauce on it)

I'm cold.

MR RANT: *You're always cold. Like your mother.*

RANT: *Can't we turn the heating up?*

MR RANT: *It costs, David. We can't have the heating on all the time.*

RANT: *Can I borrow two quid, Dad?*

MR RANT: *What for?*

RANT: *I'm going out tonight.*

MR RANT: *Where are you going, and with whom, may I ask?*

RANT: *Friends.*

MR RANT: *What friends?*

(RANT doesn't answer)

You should be working. Who are you going out with?

RANT: *Mark Cheeseman, all right?*

MR RANT: *Him! That's all you ever do. Muck about. That boy's a bad influence. Get some results at school, then you can have some fun.*

RANT:	*I get results.*
	(His father gets one of RANT's exercise books and holds it up)
MR RANT:	*That's not results. Bring some A's and B's home then you can go out. I blame your mother.*
RANT:	*Leave her out of it.*
MR RANT:	*She let you do anything. Go out. Muck about.*
	(RANT rises)
	Go on. That's right. Go to your room. Put on that stupid noise like you always do when you don't want to hear the truth.
RANT:	*I'm going out.*
MR RANT:	*I want you back by nine o'clock. Do you understand?*
RANT:	*Nine o'clock!*
MR RANT:	*What's wrong with nine o'clock?*
	(His father walks towards him angrily)
	At your age, I was back at six every night.
	(RANT goes into his room, shuts the door, and turns up the stereo.)
	Will you turn that off!
	(He shouts at the door)
	David!
	(He goes to the door)
	Open the door.
RANT:	*What do you want?*
MR RANT:	*Don't you speak to your Dad like that. Turn that racket down.*
	(RANT opens the door)
RANT:	*What?*
MR RANT:	*I can't think straight.*
RANT:	*My room, my stereo.*
MR RANT:	*Who gave you the money to buy the stereo!*

RANT: *Leave me alone. All you do is pick on me. You're always picking on me. You always pick on me.*

MR RANT: *When you have your own room in your own house —*

RANT: *O shut up!*

(MR. RANT hits him hard around the head)

The actors playing EUGENE, RANT and CHEESEY step forward and sing this song with the rest of the actors joining in its strong rhythmic backing)

LEAVE ME ALONE

EUGENE: Leave me alone
Leave me alone
I'm not crying
Just got something in my eye.

RANT: Maybe I'm not that strong.
What should I be doing?

CHEESEY: You're doing wrong.
I just can't seem to get along
With others of my kind

CHEESEY &
RANT: Oh so unkind.

EUGENE: I can see them coming,
Coming 'cross the ground.

CHEESEY &
RANT: Shut up. Shut your face. Shut up!

RANT: I'm so bad, see my muscles.
Knuckle sandwich? Taste some of this.

CHEESEY: I leave you alone, to pick up the pieces.
Go on alone.

EUGENE: Please take me home.
Please take me home.

ALL: There ain't no asylum here.
Your mother can't help you here.
ছেলেরা চলে যাও সোজা জাহান্নামে
[Go straight to hell, boys.]
Go straight to hell, boys.

SCENE 12: SAM'S REVENGE

SAM is waiting in the playground. CHEESEY enters)

SAM:	Hi,Cheesey.
CHEESEY:	All right?
SAM:	Have a good weekend?
CHEESEY:	It was all right.
SAM:	Yeah.

(She sees BECKY coming in)

There's Becky. She's really irritating me at the moment. Look at her jumper!

BECKY:	Hallo.
CHEESEY:	Hi, Beck.

(BECKY takes out a tube of peppermints and hands them round)

BECKY:	Have one.
CHEESEY:	Cheers.
SAM:	Erg! They're disgusting. Don't eat it, Cheesey. They're horrible.
CHEESEY:	Oh, try it.
SAM:	They make you go to the toilet. It says so on the packet. What's on at the pictures, Cheesey?
CHEESEY:	'Exterminator 2'.
SAM:	I wouldn't mind seeing that.
CHEESEY:	We could all go.
BECKY:	They wouldn't let us in.

(SAM turns her back on BECKY)

SAM:	Some people say stupid things, don't they? Really stupid. Really pathetic.
BECKY:	Well, they wouldn't let us in.
SAM:	Guess what, Cheesey?
CHEESEY:	What?
SAM:	I know someone who fancies Eugene.

CHEESEY:	Who?
SAM:	Not a million miles from where I'm standing.
CHEESEY:	Ooo!
	(BECKY walks off)
SAM:	We're not speaking to her.
CHEESEY:	Why?
SAM:	Cos. She hurt my feelings.
CHEESEY:	I thought she liked David.
SAM:	Not any more. But don't tell David, or he'll turn nasty. Will you? Just be sure not to tell David.
CHEESEY:	All right. Look, my brother's given me his running shoes. His feet got too big. They're a bit cut up at the sides, but they're nearly new.
SAM:	That's not fair. You'll be able to run faster than me now.
CHEESEY:	You've got to smell them.
SAM:	I'm not going to.
CHEESEY:	They're clean.
	(He tries to make her smell them)
SAM:	Aargh! Help!
	(She runs off with him following)

SCENE 13: THE VALUE OF FRIENDSHIP

EUGENE enters, walking backwards, menaced by RANT. RANT grabs him by the arm and spins him round so fast EUGENE falls. He beats him up)

RANT: *Come on, come on. Get up, mate.* Little Euge.

(He hits him on the side of his head.)

Hey, do you know what, Euge, I saw your Dad yesterday at the bus stop. He looked so well.

(EUGENE jumps to his feet and grabs a chair. He holds it above his head as if he would throw it at RANT. RANT laughs)

RANT: *Come on, do it again, do it again, go on. Do it again.*

(EUGENE lowers the chair and uses it as a shield against RANT. RANT kicks the chair)

What's all this? What's all this? Tough, are you? What's the matter? Come on, lift it up. Do something, Eugene. Ooo oooo Eugene. Go on. You ought to tell your Dad about me, Euge. Get him to come and sort me out. Next time you see him, eh? See you later.

(He laughs, and leaves. EUGENE lowers the chair, sits on it and puts his head in his hands. JO enters.)

JO: You all right? What's the matter? What's up? Have they done it again? Have they? Who is it? Was it David? You've got to report him.

EUGENE: I can't. I can't.

JO: You've got to. Report him, and he'll stop doing it.

EUGENE: It'll only make it worse.

JO: Have you told your Mum?

EUGENE: She's got enough troubles of her own.

JO: Tell her. It doesn't matter.

EUGENE: Yes, it does!

JO: Eugene, why don't you do something about it? Every day they lay into you. Every day they pick on you, don't they? You've got to do something. Why can't you?

EUGENE:	Because I don't want to.
JO:	Well, you should. It'd stop.
EUGENE:	They're not worth it.
JO:	You just get wound up, Eugene. You get so wound up and that's why they pick on you.
EUGENE:	Get lost.
JO:	So what are you going to do about it?
EUGENE:	Nothing.
JO:	What are you going to do tomorrow when it's Pass the Bogey at lunch-time?
EUGENE:	Beat them in.
JO:	But you never do.
EUGENE:	I might. Or I'll bunk off.
JO:	There are other ways, you know.
EUGENE:	Yeah, like crawling around on the floor?
JO:	No.
EUGENE:	How do you know?
JO:	Because I was bullied.
EUGENE:	When?
JO:	My first term here.
EUGENE:	All right. You know so much. Tell me how to stop them. You've got two minutes.
JO:	Yeah.
	(He acts out the following)
	Pass The Bogey. You sit in the chair that they always put in the middle. You sit there, it drops and Rant kicks you in.
EUGENE:	I don't care about him.
JO:	Yeah, but you don't show that. He thinks you do care and that's why he and his gang do it. If you didn't care, why would they do it?
EUGENE:	I want to hit him in the face.

JO: What for? It wouldn't do any good, you'll just get on report, expelled, suspended.

EUGENE: That's all right.

JO: Don.'t be stupid, Eugene.

EUGENE: David Rant said he saw my Dad at the bus stop.

(He starts to cry.)

JO: Hey, do you want to come round my house tonight? Yeah? Do you want to come to watch a video?

EUGENE: What have you got?

(There is a noise from outside. RANT returns)

RANT: Oooo Eugene! (Whispering) Careful with that chair, Eugene. Don't. Ooo, is that Eugene? Open the door. Are you in there Eugene?

(RANT enters. He is surprised to see JO there)

All right?

JO: All right.

RANT: All right, Eugene? All right, mate?

JO: Yeah, he's all right.

RANT: What's the matter, Eugene? What's the matter? Has someone upset you? What are you crying for? What you crying for, eh?

(He kicks the chair)

What you cryin' for?

JO: *Leave him alone.*

RANT: *What has it got to do with you?*

JO: What's it to do with you?

RANT: This is between me and Eugene, all right? Innit, Euge?

(He comes very close to JO)

It's got nothing to do with you. Any objections?

JO: Leave him alone.

RANT: I've written a poem for Eugene. If that's okay with you, Eugene, I'm going to read it out.

(RANT gets a piece of paper out of his pocket and starts to read)

Eugene's Dad is dead,
His mum lies alone in bed,
What does she do?
What does she see?
Eugene's Dad R.I.P.

(JO tears the paper out of his hands)

JO: Sick.

RANT: Sick?

JO: Leave him alone.

RANT: What's the matter with you two? Are you good friends with him or what?

(He looks at them)

If you want an answer, why I came back, I come back to get my coat. He's nicked my money.

(EUGENE looks at him)

Look, do you want to look?

JO: No.

RANT: Eugene Hickey's a thief. And where's my bit of paper?

(There is another dangerous pause)

Where is it?

JO: I don't know.

RANT: Where is it?

JO: You want your bit of paper?

RANT: Yeah.

(JO bends down to get it for him. As he does so, RANT kicks it away.)

You're losers, both of you. You're a waste of time.

(JO looks back steadily at him. RANT goes to EUGENE. He smiles)

I'm going to get you for this, Hickey. I'm gonna do your head in.

(RANT goes)

(As he leaves) Ooooo Eugene!

JO: You've got to do something.

(JO looks at him. EUGENE gets up out of the chair, and there is a reprise of his song)

EUGENE'S SONG AGAIN

JO: If you set the school on fire
It couldn't burn hotter than you,
And all the paper burning
Couldn't burn faster than you.

JO & EUGENE: There's a fire in my/your chest.
A fire in my/your head.

EUGENE: Don't tell me its fair.
Don't tell me to forget.

JO: But you're wriggling like a fish
A fish that's caught on a line.
So show what's inside you
But pick the right time!

If the fish shouted 'no'!
Then the line it would drop
And to all the people watching
You would call out (Everyone except Eugene)
'stop!'

SCENE 14: BECKY SPEAKS OUT

HASHI steps forward with JO.

HASHI: তারপর। ↑ [After] Sam's slumber party অবস্থার অবনতি ঘটল। আমরা কেউ বেকির সাথে কথা বললাম না। অবশেষে একদিন আমি দেখতে পেলাম বেকি কাঁদছে। [everything got worse. None of us were speaking to Becky until one day I saw she was crying and I couldn't bear being silent any longer.]

(BECKY comes on crying. She sees HASHI but doesn't expect her to   talk to her)

HASHI: Becky?

(BECKY looks up)

BECKY: Oh, it's you.

HASHI: What is it, Beck?

BECKY: Nothing.

HASHI: What is it? Tell me.

BECKY: You'd better not speak to me. You'll get into trouble.

(SAM enters)

SAM: Hashi! You'll be out of the gang.

HASHI: I don't care. She's upset.

(Hashi puts her arm round Becky)

JO: What is it, Becka? Tell us.

BECKY: They've been beating up Eugene again.

SAM: There's nothing we can do about it. It's not our business.

BECKY: I'm so tired of seeing it. I'm going to a teacher.

SAM: You can't. You'll only make things bad for yourself.

BECKY: They won't find out.

JO: Unless someone tells them.

BECKY: If you don't do something, I will. I'm going to report it to Mrs Richards.

SAM: Mrs Richards! Please. What's she going to do?

JO: She might help.

SAM:	It's been going on for weeks.
BECKY:	Someone's got to do something. Will you back me?
SAM:	In what way?
BECKY:	Say you saw it? They won't believe just me.
SAM:	I'm not going to Mrs. Richards. I mean, if you want to go to Mrs Richards, you go.
BECKY:	If you aren't willing to help, you may as well have hit him yourselves. You're scared. You won't do anything cos you're frightened.
JO:	You're frightened the next time it's going to be you.
SAM:	You go then.
BECKY:	Will you back me?
SAM:	I'll say I saw it. If I'm asked.
BECKY:	Hashi, will you back me?
HASHI:	Yeah. I will.
SAM:	Bye then. Bye, I'm going training.
	(SAM leaves)
HASHI:	SORRY.
BECKY:	ALL RIGHT.
HASHI:	ABOUT NOT SPEAKING YOU. IGNORING YOU. [I'm sorry about not speaking to you and ignoring you.] I didn't mean to go against you in support of Sam. I'm sorry.
BECKY:	It's all right. But I'm never going to forgive Sam. Ever.
HASHI:	Will you be my friend?
BECKY:	Yes.
JO:	Are you going to report it?
BECKY:	Yes. See you later.
HASHI:	Wait, Becky. I'll come with you.

SCENE 15: MRS. RICHARDS TAKES ACTION

MRS RICHARDS steps forward.

MRS RICHARDS: I was working in my class room when Becky, Hashi and Jo came to see me.

(BECKY, HASHI and JO enter)

Yes? Come in.

BECKY: MUST SPEAK YOU PRIVATE. [I must speak with you in private.]

MRS RICHARDS: What is it?

BECKY: ABOUT HAPPEN E.U.G.E.N.E. H.I.C.K.E.Y. TODAY BOYS BEAT HIM AGAIN. HAPPENED BEFORE MANY TIMES. [It's about what's happening to Eugene Hickey. The boys beat him up again today. It's happened many times before.]

MRS RICHARDS: WHO? WHO BEATING HIM? [Who? Who is beating him up?] Who? Who's been beating up Eugene?

(BECKY doesn't answer)

Hashi, do you know who it is?

(HASHI doesn't answer)

Jo? Becky, trust me. You can. Don't be frightened. If I know who it is, I can do something about it.

(BECKY and HASHI look at each other)

BECKY: D.A.V.I.D. AND OTHERS. [David. And some others.]

MRS RICHARDS: David Rant?

JO: Yes, and Mark Cheeseman but David does it more. They are saying that his dad isn't really dead.

MRS RICHARDS: Do you know where Eugene is?

JO: Yes.

MRS RICHARDS: Go and find him and ask him to come here. Thank you.

HASHI: We didn't know what to do.

MRS RICHARDS: You did the right thing. Don't worry.

BECKY: DON'T SAY OUR NAMES PLEASE. [Please don't say our names.]

MRS RICHARDS: No I won't say you told me..

(BECKY, HASHI and JO leave)

(to the audience) It wasn't long before Eugene arrived.

(EUGENE comes in, clutching his plastic bag which is torn)

Come and sit down. Are you cold? What's the matter? It's all right to talk, you can talk to me. They can't hear us so whatever you say here is between us. Are they hurting you? It's David Rant and Mark Cheeseman, isn't it?

EUGENE: They're only playing.

MRS RICHARDS: It's not playing when someone gets hurt. This is happening too often. Does your mother know about this?

EUGENE: I'm going to smash them, I'm going to smash them. What are you going to do?

MRS RICHARDS: I shall take care of it. And it will stop.

EUGENE: I want to smash them.

MRS RICHARDS: I know.

EUGENE: I want to smash them so hard.

MRS RICHARDS: I know you do but I want you to go back to the changing room and get yourself cleaned up. Do you want me to give your mother a ring?

(EUGENE shakes his head)

Do you want me to get a friend?

EUGENE: No.

MRS RICHARDS: Are you sure?

EUGENE: No.

MRS RICHARDS: Do you want to be on your own?

EUGENE: No.

MRS RICHARDS: Right. Go and get cleaned up and wait for me outside the Staff Room.

(EUGENE exits)

(To the audience) I sent for David Rant and Mark Cheeseman...

(She sets two chairs for them. RANT and CHEESEY enter)

Sit down! Who do you think you are? How long has Eugene's dad been dead? How long? How... long... has... Eugene's Dad been dead?

RANT: I don't know. I've got no idea.

MRS RICHARDS: You've got no idea?

RANT: No he didn't tell us.

MRS RICHARDS: I don't know what happened in this school before I got here, but I'm telling you this is not going on any longer. And if you don't like it, that's too bad because I'm not having it. Do you understand?

RANT: What's this about?

MRS RICHARDS: You know perfectly well what this is about. Bullying. Bullying Eugene. Now both of you are on report for two weeks. Your parents, yes, your parents will be contacted and I shall be going to visit them.

CHEESEY: But if we're on report...

MRS RICHARDS: Shut up. You are going to be watched. Watched in this class-room, in every other class-room, in the corridors, outside the school, you are going to be watched all the time. And if it happens again, you'll be out of here. Is that understood?

RANT: Yes, Mrs. Richards.

MRS RICHARDS: No more innocence. If it happens again, you're out of the school.

RANT: We were only playing, we won't do it again. That's the last time we'll do it.

MRS RICHARDS: That's right, it's the last time you do it. You're both on report so go and see the headmaster now.

CHEESEY: But if we're on report, why do we have to go and see the headmaster?

MRS RICHARDS: Because I said so.

RANT: Who's going to watch us? You said we were being watched.

MRS RICHARDS: That's right. Do you know what cruelty is?

RANT: Yes.

MRS RICHARDS: Good. That's a start. I'm not going to have you terrorise our other students in school because you're enjoying being cruel. Now go and see the headmaster now!

SCENE 16: THE WORM THAT TURNED.

A wet lunchtime. EUGENE is on his own, reading. BECKY enters with her diary.

EUGENE: Hi, Becky.

BECKY: Anyone sitting here?

(BECKY sits down and starts to write in her diary)

EUGENE: What are you writing?

BECKY: Just my diary. I was too tired to write it last night.

EUGENE: You'll never guess what happened last night.

BECKY: What?

EUGENE: David Rant's Dad came round to speak to my mother.

BECKY: Why?

EUGENE: He came to say sorry about —

(SAM enters)

SAM: Oooh what's happening here? Are you two going out with each other or something? Come on, tell us.

(CHEESEY enters)

Becky's in love. Oh, you look in love. Oh Becky, I forgot. I want to tell you something.....

(SAM snatches BECKY'S diary)

Oh hang on, hang on. What night are you seeing him, Becky?

BECKY: Sam, can I just have that back.

SAM: (Pretending to read the diary) Oh interesting.

BECKY: Give it back, Sam, give it back.

SAM: Becky's getting upset.

BECKY: Give it back, Sam, give it back.

(HASHI, JO, and RANT enter. SAM throws the diary to CHEESEY)

RANT: Cheesey, Cheesey, Cheesey!

(CHEESEY throws it to RANT)

BECKY: Please David give it back.

JO: (To EUGENE) Are you all right? What's going on?

(EUGENE Nods)

BECKY: Give it back.

(SAM looks over RANT'S shoulder at the open diary)

RANT: Thursday night.

SAM: Ooooh! What's happening on Thursday night?

BECKY: Nothing. Give it back.

SAM: It must be love.

EUGENE: Stop it.

RANT: What is it with you?

EUGENE: Stop it. Really funny that, reading someone else's diary. Really funny innit, David.

SAM: Just because she's your girlfriend.

EUGENE: You got it wrong then, haven't you?

SAM: (Reading) What's this? 'I think Rant and Cheesey and Sam are just big stupid bullies and I'd like to see what would happen to them if their father died.'

(JO goes over to them and takes the diary)

JO: Give it here.

(JO gives it back to BECKY. RANT makes a move towards him but is stopped by EUGENE)

EUGENE: Sometimes I lie awake all night just laughing at how funny you lot are.

RANT: Well go laugh then, don't tell me about it. Go take your girlfriend with you, you big mouth, who talks to teachers.

BECKY: Come on, David, leave it.

RANT: This is nothing to do with you Beck.

BECKY: Yes, it does. It was me. I told Mrs. Richards.

SAM: Be quiet Becky.

HASHI: I went too. Me and Jo. We backed her.

(She looks at JO)

Didn't we?

JO:	Yeah.
HASHI:	It was us that told on you, David and you knew all about it, Sam.
BECKY:	You said you'd back us. If asked.
SAM:	I never!
BECKY:	Sam, you might as well tell the truth.
SAM:	So what? (To BECKY and HASHI) I thought you were my friends.
RANT:	Ooo Eugene. You little trouble-maker.
EUGENE:	You don't know what you're doing is a waste of time.
RANT:	So you're saying I'm a waste of time.
JO:	I'm saying that too, Dave.
CHEESEY:	Me too. Sorry Dave.
RANT:	Do you want me to bust your nose? Aren't you scared?
EUGENE:	Yes, I'm scared of this...
	(He points to RANT'S fist)
	...but I'm no longer afraid of you, David. Yeah, anyone can have a joke when you pull my hair or something like that. But I hope one day you'll start listening to people. Cos there's a lot to learn. Not about what someone puts in their diary, but about how people are and what they say to us.
RANT:	You don't know the half of it.
	(He turns to go)
	(The bell rings and everyone goes off except for RANT who calls EUGENE back)
RANT:	Eugene.
EUGENE:	Yeah?
RANT:	Come back.
EUGENE:	All right. What?
RANT:	I don't want you telling anyone this...
EUGENE:	What's that?
RANT:	Even Cheesey doesn't know.

EUGENE:	What?
RANT:	Before we started school, the First Year, my Mum died.
EUGENE:	I know. Your Dad told us last night.
RANT:	When we found out what happened to you, I was really angry with you, Eugene. You didn't come and tell us.
EUGENE:	I couldn't, could I? They just don't know.
RANT:	They don't, do they? You're supposed to forget about it.
EUGENE:	You don't forget about it.
RANT:	No. Like after a while, after everyone's said their bits, you're left on your own. About what I did though. I'm sorry.
EUGENE:	Yeah.
RANT:	I mean it.
EUGENE:	You don't have to be sorry. Yes, you do. You made me feel my life wasn't worth living.
RANT:	Yeah.
EUGENE:	Yeah.

(EUGENE exits towards everyone else and Rant, after a moment's hesitation, goes off the other way on his own. Everyone steps forward for the final song which is reprise of the opening song of the play:)

FINAL SONG

Who's going to say it's not funny
When you know that a joke is causing pain?
Who's going to move away from the crowd
And say 'let's not do it again'?

তোমরা এখন বন্ধু হবে। তোমরা জানো কিভাবে।
[Just be friendly now. You know how.]
JUST FRIENDLY NOW. YOU KNOW HOW.
Just be friendly now. You know how.

If you look in all the corners
You'll find someone's trying to hide.
It's much harder when you've got no friends
So don't leave people outside.

Open the circle now. Now. Now. Now.
দলের চক্র দাও খুলে এক্ষুনি, এক্ষুনি, এক্ষুনি, এক্ষুনি।
[Open the circle now. Now. Now. Now.]
OPEN CIRCLE NOW. NOW. NOW. NOW.

It isn't true that kids are always cruel.
And others just won't care.
Don't keep bullying a secret,
In your heart you know it's not fair.

Let other people in. LET THEM JOIN.
Let other people in.
ওদের দলে ঢুকতে দাও।
[Let them join.]
Let other people in. LET THEM JOIN!

THE END

THE LETTERS

The work of the company was featured in two Thames *Help!* Programmes in June, and a BBC Forty Minutes Documentary on bullying in November 1989.

As a result of these programmes we received many letters from young and older people whose experiences of bullying had left them with deep and painful memories. They have given us permission to use their testimony in our work, and in this section we publish seven of the letters in slightly shortened versions.

Also included are some letters to the Young Guardian, written following a feature on Bullying by Melanie MacFadyean which reviewed *Only Playing, Miss*.

Dear Penny Casdagli,

From about the 2nd year of my secondary school education I was bullied, physically and mentally. Being quite short I was an easy target when other boys wanted to show their superiority. If at this point I had summoned up the courage to fight back, my school career may have been different. But there was always something inside holding me back.

At about this time a boy called Stuart joined the school. When he was on his own he was quite reasonable, but a group of boys were taken in by him being loud-mouthed, and used to follow him around. He had certain rituals which sound absurd now, but were infuriating then: he'd call me 'Little R', saying it in a pathetic voice, and at the same time pushing my head sideways violently. He would do this 20 times a day. It sounds silly now, but this would happen 5 days a week for 3 years. At break times he would grab me by the wrists and kick my legs away. He would then start to spin around and let go so I flew in the air and fell on the floor. It wasn't that this was just painful, you see everyone would watch, so they knew Stuart was walking all over me. Hence no-one respected me.

As for my own school career, it suffered quite badly - I spent more time worrying about how to get through the next week than I did on my homework. In the fifth year I never raised the issue of whether to stay at school or get a job: leaving school meant leaving the bullying. So in June I left one Friday and started work on the Monday.

Stuart did not do very well in his exams and was forced to leave school as well. It's now 2 years since I left school. I have found the experiences I went through can sometimes lead me to being unreasonable. If it is apparent to me that someone is acting in a dominating manner towards me, I am wary of them and usually rude...

Dear Madam,

I was bullied at school from the age of 13 to 16. I was constantly harassed and teased and called all the names under the sun. My hair was pulled, I was kicked, punched and followed by the same gang whenever they saw me.

It all started when I made friends with a very poor girl because I felt sorry for her. She used to bring jam sandwiches to school every day. She was picked on very badly, often being beaten to the floor and punched and kicked in the stomach. Don't think that girls are more gentle than boys when bullying, at times they can be worse.

Because I was a bit of a truanter at school, I used to skip lessons and even whole days at a time. That was mostly because I couldn't stand to be in the class with the bullies.

Then one day some girls told me that a friend of the bully, who was older than me, wanted to have a fight. Of course I said I didn't want to have a fight with anyone. They started crowding round me. I fought to get out of the crowd, but there she was standing there.

'I want to fight you,' she said. I told her I didn't want a fight. She kept pushing me until my bones were shaking. Then she said something about me not having a Dad. I could ignore her no longer. And before I realized, we were really fighting.

I hurt her really badly: her face was cut, she had a black eye, also some of her hair was pulled out. It's funny because I had long hair and I didn't lose any. I didn't want to carry on fighting as I have a condition that no doctor has been able to diagnose: after a lot of physical activity, like running, or like when I was fighting, my hands become numb and I get so tired I can't carry on.

After that fight the girls left me alone, and even started being friendly, but I just ignored them...

I'm now married and have a boy of my own, called Yusuf. I just hope that when he gets to school age bullying will have disappeared.

Dear Madam,

After watching the 'Help!' programme, I decided to write to you with my own experience of bullying.

I've just left school now, but when I was in the 3rd year at school, me and another girl had a row with five or six other members of our 'group'. They didn't like it because we sat on the field to eat our lunch instead of going to the canteen. I know it sounds really silly, but because of this my friend and I were made outcasts. One day however they came up to me and asked me to go round with them again, but without my other friend. I said no, because it's not fair to leave one person on their own.

However, before I knew it, I was on my own, because Natalie had gone back with them and left me.

It was here that all my troubles began. I had always been very popular at school, but one by one my friends stopped talking to me. I spent my days wandering around on my own, just waiting to go home to my family in the evening. I used to dread English lessons because the class was all together and I felt like an intruder. I lost all confidence to speak out in class for fear of being jeered at.

It all came to a head one day in English when one particularly tough girl, Suzanne, decided that she wanted to sit in my seat. I was terrified as she and a few girls started shouting at me. The teacher came in just as Suzanne threw the desk at me. The teacher was useless, she just sent her out and I was left to suffer the laughter from other members of the form.

Shortly afterwards Suzanne got expelled, which made matters worse for me. I was made to feel that it was my fault, although I knew it wasn't because she was always in trouble.

By this time my family was suffering as well as me: my sister was getting hassle as she went to the same school, and my Mum and Dad were feeling the pressure.

It went on like this right the way through the 4th year. By the 5th year I was so depressed that I talked to a teacher, who tried to convince me that it was my fault and that I was imagining a lot of it. She really upset me, and one day, after a particularly bad day I walked out of school.

Anyhow my Mum and Dad saw the Head and she talked to us all separately, and after this it got a lot better. But by this time it was too late because I was leaving school shortly.

This small group of girls gradually turned the majority of my year group against me, and my school life was made a misery. I have however come through it all, and have become stronger for the experience. Bullying is a terrible thing whether it be mental or physical. Writing it all out has helped me to come to terms with it.

Dear Sir,

...I have a hatred of people, especially children, being bullied. My ex was not a bully at school at school, but turned into one when we got married. He used physical and mental bullying. We divorced when my daughter was 2 years old. She is now 6.

As I was trying to write down the address as we watched the programme, my daughter said: 'Rip that up. I'm not being bullied!' But as her mother, I know she is...

It takes many forms. Hers started out as two pairs of glasses in one week, broken — she tells me accidentally. Secondly her friends are not playing with her. She hates seeing anyone fighting in or out of school.

A victim's parents do not know how to cope... some of her answers would tell you she is a victim, but one who takes it out on me. Ironically, I wish she was a bully. Well what's best for a child — being a victim or the bully?

Dear Sirs,

Doesn't it fire the anger again, and so strongly too, seeing other people go through it. I have been there and for once I can now open up this dark corner of my life.

During my primary education in a somewhat privileged school....other children saw us (my brother went there too) as definitely not like them... Despite consolation from concerned parents we felt no better about our 'better' position in life. The bullying started... not on a grand scale, but on any level this is sickening.

Grammar school passed off well... until I moved to Reading at the age of fifteen. Sheer hell ensued for over a year, and I consider that time to be the saddest of my life.

For reasons which I still do not understand... I was labelled a Jew although I am not one... This worked through the whole of my year. Even to a cousin of mine, who I suppose rather than be the odd one out had to join in. I can never forgive him the relish with which he used to incite the whole coach-load of kids to chant about me.

There were maybe two people during this period who were in my year and who were kind. My heart used to lift when I saw them. If only to have someone to talk to who wasn't going to humiliate and ridicule me. They made me feel that little bit safer.

Monday nights left me feeling sick and in complete dread of the next day Tuesday—Jewsday. I remember this starting up in one pottery class: I held my head low hoping I might somehow hide within myself and become invisible. The pottery master tried to quell the chorus. I just wanted to cry long and loud.

On the playing fields the physical side took over, the result of which was always some bruising. It was considered great sport if they could bring me down mentally as well as physically. I eventually gave up sport and claimed the art rooms as sanctuary.... I felt quite pleased that I managed to make a change to my life that did some good.

I remember... a girl in my tutor group one afternoon got up from her chair and zig-zagged through the desks to where I was sitting. Above her head in her right hand, like a trophy, she held some cardboard money. 'Don't spend it all at once, Jew' And the thing was placed in the middle of my desk.

Graffiti was ever prominent: my desk, chair, books and locker were all marked in indelible black marker that they belonged to a Jew.

Academically I lost out. At the time when exams were all important my life was taken over by something like self-preservation. I had no stamina left.

Although the bullying eventually stopped, I could never have made friends with anyone there. I still cannot take criticism, effrontery, sarcasm etc. The negative sides of people's attitudes in conversation I always feel are being levelled at me. I have to keep myself in check. This I attribute totally to the constant attack I was under in my important years.

I have just taken a deep breath, and feel a little better that I can tell someone else.

Dear Ms Casdagli,

From the first day at Secondary School I was bullied in a day to day routine of sadistic violence.

Dave and Barry were firm friends and worked together sharing the fun they derived from inflicting pain on me. They were happy, well-adjusted boys from a stable family background. The bullying was a trend which made them feel powerful and 'cock' of the school. Which in our last year, of course, they were.

They were not bullies in the true sense of the word because, to my knowledge, I was the only one they persecuted. They had fights and won them, they were popular, they were even protective of younger and weaker boys. They drifted through school unconcerned about my pain and anguish.

David H was a different character altogether. He was a loner whose love of inflicting savage pain on anyone younger and weaker gave him a thrill. There was never any escape and not submitting only made it worse.

I felt it was my fault anyway. I was tall, thin, wore glasses, introverted, artistic, hated sport and spoke with a London accent (we were in Lancashire). I wouldn't cry either, and this spurred him on to greater efforts.

I couldn't tell my parents because a complaint would have resulted in reprisals. The teaching staff were well aware of what was going on but chose to consider it as an acceptable part of school life. Their belittling sarcasm only acted as encouragement to the bully.

My schoolwork suffered because my time was spent on how best to escape after class. All this has taught me a lot about children that I have never forgotten - which often happens when we grow up.

I became a Residential Social Worker in special schools and children's homes. I realize now that my childhood experiences had developed in me a deep concern for the deprived child and an obligation to offer help. Bullying is something I am constantly on the lookout for... If somebody is disliked by the majority, or is getting it unfairly in the neck, then I jump in as a friend and ally.

I have lived and worked, laughed and cried with 196 children in care for 18 years, and if the experiences of my childhood served to enhance theirs, then it wasn't a high price to pay.

Dear Ms Casdagli,

I would be swinging on the swing, minding my own business, when they would come over and hit me. I found this upsetting because I was always told by my mum and dad that if you were to be hit, it was because you had done wrong. I couldn't understand what I had done to deserve this treatment in the park. When I used to tell my parents, they would just say 'hit them back', but I found this to be alien to my nature. It did not make sense.

I can remember one day.. two big blokes of about 12 were tormenting me in the park. When my Mum saw what was happening she ran out screaming at the two boys to leave me alone. I felt a bit annoyed at her for doing this, as I was beginning to see it in a different light. I think that at times I used to give my Mum and Dad hell just to make them hit me, so that I would at least get some attention. I often wonder if I used to do this with the bullies. Sometimes I think perhaps something inside me wants to be attacked.

When I went to school I was beaten up nearly every day. But nobody did anything about it. I was good at putting a brave face on it. I was brought up to be hard, a real man. If I cried, my Dad would hit me until I stopped the 'nonsense' as he called it. When I was a child I didn't think that I had anyone on my side. I must add that I am gay, as I'm sure that this has something to do with my bullying.

I didn't really have any friends. I had one so-called friend who, when the mood took him, would bash me up. But I always went back with him as I knew he was OK most of the time.

When I got to about 15 I found I was losing my ability to laugh it off. I started to feel really miserable. I used to get a pen and break the clip off so there was a nasty sharp bit, and I used to damage myself with it. Also I used to bite my hands so that it would really hurt. The teeth marks would be left in them.

The thing that really hurt me was that some girls from the same school, who I thought were sensible and kind, started to laugh at me for being pushed around, and even joined in on the jeering. I kept saying 'Why me, why should I have to put up with all this?' I wanted to commit suicide. I don't think I had cried for about 8 years before this (I was told by my parents that men don't cry). The only thing that stopped me was that by this time I was beginning to suffer from agoraphobia: at home time my insides would go over and I didn't want to walk the way home.

I wish to God now that I had never gone to school... it makes me sick to think about it. How good and well-behaved I was. But I found it pointless trying to do well at school as the others would always rip up my books etc.

The reason I never took the bullying issue any further was because I was made to feel that it was all my own fault for not being hard and hitting back.

Even now, if I was to be set on in the street, I would feel more angry at myself than at the yobs.

I don't know what it was. Perhaps it was something in me that bullies could identify with. I've often felt that it's just their way of communicating with me. Or could it be that I'm soft and gentle, the opposite to what they are? I don't know...

Following Melanie McFadyean's article in the Young Guardian (6 December 1989), several more pieces about bullying were published on that page during the subsequent months. We would like to thank the contributors and the *Guardian* for giving permission to use the following letters:

At my last school a boy never missed a chance to make jibes at me. Whenever I tried to speak or voice my opinion, he would make snide remarks under his breath, or jokes about my 'relationship' with our female teacher. I found this very distressing and was so nervous that I was unable to speak in class without bursting into tears.

The desire to make yourself look 'big' in front of others is another aspect of bullying. The same boy would, when he encountered me with his older friends, make me the object of their hilarity.

I felt I should ally myself with him, I actually admired him. So partly to impress him and partly to make myself look big in front of some of the others — people who couldn't care less whether I lived or died—I began to torment a first-year boy who got on the same bus as me. I was in the third year at the time. They were pathetic things I did to him — banging his head on the window, sliding his bag from under his seat, tripping him up as he walked by. It reached the point where he was afraid to set foot on the on the coach because the day before I had threatened to get him. His parents complained to the school and to my parents. This gave me a deep shock, I was unaware how distressed he was. I learned that it is not easy to know how deeply you injure someone.

To me, my bullying had been a pathetic attempt to hide my true personality behind a show of 'face', but to him it had been a traumatic and disturbing experience.

I realised that most bullies, myself included, are insecure and frightened of showing their true feelings and personality so they take refuge behind a screen, they torment others, thinking this improves their image amongst their peers. I learned that the truth is the opposite of that and to my cost one or two of my friends looked down on me. In effect I was bullying myself.

Male, 15.

One aspect of bullying is that of pupil by teacher. To abuse a position of trust is unforgiveable and I have personal knowledge of how humiliating it can be.

It began in the third year when I was 14. Self-esteem is not very high at this age and repeated put-downs cut deep. The first incident was when a new teacher filled in for a games lesson. It soon became clear that she didn't know the rules of rounders; I'm not the sort of person who takes games overly seriously but, mildly irritated, I muttered that she wasn't doing things properly.

At first it didn't click. I loved sport and knew I was good but, in the continuing absence of our regular teacher, I was dropped from teams, goals scored went unappreciated, while other people were given preference in such things as booking courts. Then the comments began.

'You needn't be so pleased with yourself, any fool could have scored from there,' and, 'Wouldn't the rounders expert prefer to take this lesson?' Even when I was joking with friends about playing mixed hockey: 'I suppose that would be your only chance to impress the boys.' A juvenile remark, but stinging to an adolescent girl.

Things came to a head one lunch break: her remark about my new haircut 'helping me look almost normal' was too much for my battered pride. 'Why the hell can't you leave me alone?' I yelled, but I hadn't bargained for the delight she took in her whiplash answer.

'Oh well, that's typical of you. There are things written in the staffroom about you young lady — you're well known and don't you forget it.'

It emerged later this was nothing more dramatic than a note mentioning my mother was in hospital and I might be finding things difficult. That retort and its damage remains with me even now as I recall the pain and shock it provoked. During the time of her persecution and for weeks afterwards I became with-drawn and miserable, inwardly terrified about what she might say next.

My experience was soul-destroying. However, if it happened to someone 'straight' like me, how must others more rebellious or outspoken suffer? I've seen others, especially boys, bullied unmercifully by teachers thinking they are having a bit of fun. But I know that this 'fun', when persistent and pointed, causes as much misery and distress as pupil-pupil bullying that teachers condemn and claim to abhor.

I was bullied between the ages of nine and 16. They called me a 'boffin' and a 'lessy'. They punched me so hard in the stomach that I fell to my knees and was, for a few moments, oblivious of everything except the pain.

The first day I wore a new coat to school, they pushed me so that I fell on a muddy and oily track — the coat never came clean. When some dinner-money went missing, they accused me of stealing it. I was the last person picked for the hockey and netball teams. I became so miserable that I developed stomach pains and was admitted to hospital for suspected diabetes.

The bullying interfered with my adolescence; I was 15 before my periods started. Sick of being mocked for answering questions, I became resolutely silent in class. Ridicule of my clothes made me shun fashion. I stopped reading for four years; I didn't want to grow up.

The bullying stopped when I went to sixth form college. The bullies either stayed in the school's sixth form or left. Nobody at college accused me of being a 'boffin' or a 'stuck-up cow'. It was all right for me to work hard, and being boyfriendless didn't matter: I was accepted.

I was bullied because the children with influence considered that my voice, background, clothes and appearance were all wrong. I hold our pernicious class system responsible for the wretchedness of my school life.

The bullying I received was mostly verbal. The cliche 'sticks and stones may break my bones but words will never hurt me' was never any comfort. Words have left me a nervous adult, awkward about the way I talk, afraid to express opinions and scared of other people. Bullying can have lasting consequences.

THE WORKSHOP WRITINGS

Neti-Neti decided it was not enough just to tour *Only Playing, Miss* in schools. Our audience of 11 to 14 year-old schoolchildren needed to be given a chance to have their say. And so, with the help of The Sir John Cass's Foundation, writing workshops were set up in ten ILEA Secondary Schools. These were both a preparation for the play and a chance to explore the issue of bullying through multilingual drama, song, tape-recordings, video and writings in English, Bengali and BSL. They were enabled by Francis Gobey of Neti-Neti.

We would like to thank Tunmarsh and Oak Lodge Schools for the Deaf, and Central Foundation Girls', Dick Sheppard, Fulham Cross, North Westminster, Sacred Heart, Sir John Cass, and Sir William Collins Secondary Schools for their participation in the workshop programme, not forgetting the individual teachers whose support and advice made the workshops so fruitful.

The writings are arranged to follow the journey of the workshops. We start with ourselves, our feelings and our place in the world. We look at the power that others have over us and we have over them. We reflect on our varied experiences of the behaviour called 'bullying'. Building on this, we explore the difficult choices we all face whenever bullying is going on. Finally we offer advice and celebrate our positive uniqueness and communal strength.

In the words of one participant in a workshop drama: *If you get it out in the open, you've got more chance of solving it.*

WORKSHOP WRITINGS

Feelings

Through drama we can get in touch with our own strong feelings and come to terms with them in other people. Feelings are things we have in common: there are times we all feel happy, sad, brave, scared, angry, jealous... But feelings are also very much our own. Here are some of the feelings we shared in the workshops.

I once hid what I really felt about someone: I fancied a boy but could not tell anyone about it, not even my best friend.

I once told the truth even though it was difficult. Because my Mum moved to Yugoslavia, and she has been there for one month, last night I missed her. I did not want to tell my Dad, just in case he got upset. But he didn't. And I phoned my Mum.

I was jealous when my cousin got something and I wanted it badly: it was a beautiful doll.

I was happy when Arsenal won 2-0 vs Liverpool and also Arsenal won the League cup. And when Liverpool won I was devastated.

I felt sad when I broke my leg and had to go to hospital because I get scared in hospitals.

The last time I got really angry was yesterday. My sister started coming feisty so I beat her up and I got the blame for it.

I felt sad a long time ago. I was tired every day. My Daddy was smacking me a long time. I stayed in my bedroom. A long time ago.

My sister opened the door and the dog ran away. I felt angry with my sister. The dog came back the next day. I felt happy.

All the other pupils looked at me. I looked at all of them. In my mind they looked like bullies and my heart was beating wildly. I felt embarrassed. A deaf person asked: 'What's your name?' ... I was not embarrassed afterwards.

I was jealous of my friend's computer, and kept moaning at my mother for a computer one day.

I am weak I am strong

After looking at the times we felt brave and confident and the times we felt scared and vulnerable we wrote a song together. This is part of it.

I am weak I am strong
Please don't leave me on my own

When I feel miserable
is when I see my best
friend going off with someone
else. And I've got no-one
to play with and I'm left
alone. These are the times
I feel weak.

When I feel happy
is when I've got high
marks in a test. And
when my friends are all
around me. And they
share everything with
me. These are the times
I feel strong.

When I feel sad
or when I've been bad
It's times like this I feel weak

When I'm weak
I don't like
being on my own.
When I'm strong
really nothing
can go wrong.

I'm happy when I'm home and safe.
Then I'm happy with my life.
I am weak I am strong
Please don't leave me on my own.

Who has power over me?

In this exercise we looked at the power some people have over us, and how they used it.

Who has power over me?
Parents, family, teachers, sometimes friends, relatives, the government, sometimes bullies.

What power?
To tell me what to do and when, what's right, what's for my own good. Power to make me understand and learn. To tell us what to do and put us in the right when we are wrong. My Mum and Dad have the power of love and kindness.

Do they use it well?
In a way yes because they teach us how to respect others; yes sometimes, because they want you to respect them. Some parents use force and some talk to you about it.

What power do they not have?
To kick me out of the house until I am a certain age; to hit me, disown me; stop me from what I want to be in the future; chuck me out of home. They can't tell us what to dream and think and feel and do in some cases. They do not have the power to make me eat what I don't want, to force me to do what they want me to do.

Does anyone have that power?
No; yes and it is God. No-one else; no-one; my sister, the people around me who have power over me.

What kind of power does the bully have?
Well, Y thought that X was the leader of the group, but just over some people in the class. He thought that he told people what to do, and could ignore them or exclude them. He had a sort of gang and could get other people to do the dirty work. It's not all the time though. I don't really think that he is bullying. He's never really done it to me, but he's got power over some people in the class... The weird thing is he doesn't really have that much power over kids shorter than him; it's the ones that are taller than him that he has power over. It's really funny.

And you?
If one of my friends was being hurt, if I saw someone being bullied, I would go and help them. I feel very confident in myself.

Friends and enemies

What do we want from our friends? What do we fear in our enemies?

A friend is an enemy and a friend is someone who can be kind to you.

I want my best friend to like me and to be nice. And not to be selfish. And to help me do my work when I'm stuck.

A friend is someone who can be on my side wherever I go.

I want my best friend to be kind and not selfish. And to help me with my problems.

An enemy is someone I don't feel bad about hurting.

A friend is someone who is always on my side, whatever I do.

An enemy is someone I want to be friends with who doesn't want to be friends with me.

I want to be friends with Elizabeth, but she doesn't want to be mine.

A friend is someone I can be angry with and they don't stop being my friend. A friend is my teacher. I would like a friend that is kind.

My best friend I would like to be trusting, with a sense of humour, someone who doesn't lie, trusting.

There was a boy called Eric and I really hated him. He was scum and we had a fight and it was a draw, but I didn't feel bad about it.

An enemy is someone who is always hurting me or I'm hurting them.

Have you ever..?

It is not easy to decide what is and what is not 'bullying'. We used a questionnaire to think about what we have done and what has happened to us. Here are our stories of being picked on, teased, called names, excluded from the group, insulted and hurt. But have we done these things to other people too?

One day I teased this first-year boy about his ruck-sack because everybody was acting as though he was the king. He kept being feisty to me and my friends, so I said to him:

'Is that a parachute on your back?' and he was really upset.

The New Kid

It was the second day of the new term. We were in class. Suddenly there was a knock on the door. There was a new boy who wanted to join our class. His name was Paul. He was about six foot tall. He was very lonely. It was lunchtime; me and my friends were playing football. The new boy Paul came and just kicked the ball away and swore at us:

'Why don't you let me play?'

My friend said:

'Because you didn't tell us that you wanted to play with us.'

The new boy began arguing with us. Then my friend said:

'Today at home-time we are going to beat you up.'

Then at home-time we beat the new boy up.

In the Dinner Queue

A: Look! There's a new kid.

K: And he is in the front of the queue. Come on. Let's push in.

S: Oi! Don't push in.

K: You're a Firsty.

A: What's your name?

S: Stewart.

A: Stewpot!

(A fight breaks out. Karl intervenes)

K: All right mate.

(Fight stops)

One day a group of kids started picking on my friend and me, all because we wouldn't give them some dinner money. They beat us up badly and the teacher would do nothing about it because she didn't believe me. So in the end I walked into school badly beaten up. It was then and only then that the teacher did something about it. The kids got suspended.

One day at lunchtime two sixth-former boys told me to go somewhere. I said no, but they said:

*'You ***.'*

'Back to you,' I said.

Then they wanted to hit me. Then I told them I would tell the teacher. That's the end. I told the teacher and the boys got detention.

Q: Have they bullied you again?

A: No. They said they wouldn't do it to me again. They promised me.

Q: Did you feel good?

A: Yes.

Q: Did you feel strong?

A: YES!

Q: Have you ever been bullied again?

A: No.. Yeah I have... by loads of people.

Q: And how do you feel about it?

A: Sad.

Once I sided with someone who was being picked on by a group because she never fights back, and is always on her own.

We were in PE. Everyone started to pick on Steve because he had grassed on Festus — about ripping up a lot of paper. They all said:

'What did you have to grass for?' everyone was shouting.

I came from the changing-room and said:

'Don't shout at him. He's O.K.'

I did this because he was my good friend. Everyone stopped. After I'd done it I felt that I could control the class; they were under my orders. I felt powerful.

Today my friends were teasing me about my Nike Air...

I was bullied by someone in my class in Primary School. I was quite young then, about six or seven. It was mainly racism because the other boy was black, and he didn't like people like me, because I come from Bangladesh. And he used to beat me up every day after school. And then he left the school. Everything was O.K. then. I wasn't bullied again.

My thing was similar to hers, the same racism thing. But I wasn't like scared. I knew I could get the girl back... not then, but in the future. And I did get her back.

I remember when Michelle was picking on me. She called me names, and beat me up. My Dad said:

    'If you beat my daughter up I'll beat you up.'

When she went home I tripped her up, and she said:

    'Wait till I get you.'

    'I will wait for you in the park after school,' I said.

But she was not there, so I went home. She knocked at my door and my Dad answered it, and Michelle said:

    'Is Emma there?'

    'Yes. Wait a minute,' said my Dad.

So Michelle waited outside for me. When I went out there, she said:

    'Shall we carry on with the fight?'

    'Yes,' I said. I beat her up and she went home crying to her Mum.

The Bully Kids' Gang

There was a girl called Sabba. Her eyes used to change into different colours. Once we saw her eyes go rusty orange, grey and green. She was a tell-tale and a trouble-maker too. She used to go to the Mosque. She used to say to the teacher that we hit her. But we didn't really.

One day she got us into real trouble. We had to write 'I won't hit Sabba again' 25 times in Bengali. That made us really mad. We made a plan that we were going to bash her up when we found her alone.

It was our Arabic holiday for one week. That week we saw her alone, walking along the pavement. We were hiding by the dustbin. We saw her skinny figure coming towards us. Then we went near her and we surrounded her. We were acting like cool people or badboys.

We could see Sabba's body shaking like a mad cat. Then we said:

'CAT'S EYES. Don't show off next time!'

We punched her three times on the bones. And then she started to cry. She said that she would tell her Uncle Gozza Hazi. We said that we didn't care if she told her bendy Gozza Hazi. Then we gave her the ticket of our gang — a skull and crossbones with the word Dead! written on it — and said: 'Keep it, so you can remember that we are cool.' Then the dog chased us. We ran and just left her then. We don't know what happened to her.

Illness

I thought everything would be the same when I got back to school, with people saying: Look everybody! Dwayne is back!. I thought it would be even better than before.

But that was not to be. Instead, they said:

'Oh, there is Dwayne.'

Then as the day went on I realized there was a new 'badboy' in our class: Winston. Winston was supposed to be my best friend, but now he had taken my role in the class and my girlfriend, Nicole, as well. This was too much!

Then Winston started to crack one of the jokes I'd made, and everybody laughed except me. I told a joke — one that Winston had laughed at months before — only to hear a sudden silence. Then the pips went and I ran home as quick as I could.

The next day I wore my 'baddest' trainers, the ones I usually wear to the disco and hip-hop gigs, only to find everybody wearing dungarees and Kickers. Turquoise Kickers!

I remember when I used to cuss people with kickers and now they were in fashion. So I went up to my older sister, who was wearing a pair of old people's shoes, and I said:

'What are they called?'

'They're called Wallabies,' she said. 'And they're in fashion. And you're not. So will you turn around and walk away slowly, and don't look back.'

I now realized what the problem was: I was out of fashion. When I was ill my stupid sister didn't tell me was what on the fashion scene.

DILEMMAS

When faced with a bully we often don't know what to do: one part of us is strong inside and tells us we can cope, another part of us is scared and tells we can't. We are both frightened and brave. In these short plays you can see what is going on in a person's mind — as two 'angels' give me advice about what to do.

Inside my head

Me: Oh no he's coming. What shall I do?

A1: Run. Run.

A2: Stand up to him. Fight him, hit him! Don't let it go on!

A1: You can't take on all of them. There's got to be twenty of them there.

A2: Come on. You've got to stand up. He'll come after you all your life. Come on now.

Me: There's not twenty of them there.

A1: There are. It doesn't matter how many of them there are. There's more than you. You're on your own...

A2: Don't listen to him. He's a coward himself. You don't want to be a coward. A1: I'm not a coward.

A2: Yes you are. Always running away.

A1: Yes but you've just got to run. You're going to lose all your pocket money on the first day you've got it.

Me: Then he won't come back to him again.

A1: He will though, because he'll know that he can get more pocket money.

A2: Listen to me, listen! If you stand up to him he won't come back. (the voices argue)

The Bully's Friend

Me: I wonder if I should tell the teacher. Michael's probably my best friend. I don't know what to do. What shall I do?

A1: Go and tell.

A2: Nah, don't tell. He might beat you up.

Me: I could have him any time. I don't know why I should be scared of him.

A1: You shouldn't be scared of anyone see. Stand up to bullies.

A2: I don't think you can beat him up.

Me: It doesn't matter if I can't beat him up. If I go to the teacher, he'll sort him out quickly.

A1: Yes that's true. Teachers can always do things.

Me: I don't know what to do.

A2: It's up to you. Me: I'm going to tell. That's it.

The Bully

Me: What shall I do?

A1: Bully her.

A2: Why do you do it?

A1: Fight her.

A2: Don't do it. You'll get into trouble.

Me: Right!

A1: Fight.

A2: Let's go home. Please go home.

A1: Don't go home. Bully her!

Me: Wait. I can't think any more.

Bully and Teacher

B: I wonder what she's got me in here for.

A1: She's going to expel you isn't she?

A2: No she's not. If you are good she's not going to expel you.

T: Oh. What shall I do to him?

A1: Just tell him to get out of the school. Don't give him any chances.

T: I have to give him a fair chance.

A2: Be really gentle with him. I know people like that. They won't do it again. Give him a chance.

A1: No don't. He's a nasty sort.

T: Are you sure about this?

A1: Listen to me not her.

A1: Give him a chance.

PROBLEM PAGE

When talking to yourself isn't solving your problem, talking or writing to someone else can help.

Dear Georgette,

My best friend is a bully. She keeps on picking on a girl in our class. She says it's just for a laugh, but I think it is quite serious.

The girl that is picked on is a loner. I've never seen her smile, and I've often seen her cry by herself in a corner. The girl has missed a lot of school and I think that my friend is the cause. I feel sorry for her and would like to help. But I don't want to lose my friend.

Please help. A concerned friend

Georgette says...

You should try telling your bully friend to stop. Ask her why she dislikes this girl so much. If it doesn't work, tell an adult and hopefully this unkindness with your friend and classmate will be stopped. Talk to the girl and try to find out her feelings.

Dear Problem Page,

I am being bullied at school. I have told my parents, but they just tell me to stick up for myself and stand up to him. I am too scared to tell the teacher who is doing it in case that person beats me up again.

This boy takes most of my dinner money because he doesn't get any. Every day he empties my bag, turning it upside down in front of everybody —

making me look a fool. He makes me do all his homework. He's in my class and I always lend him pens.

The teacher doesn't notice, or when she does, she thinks he is mucking about. Please, please, please help me.

Jo. London.

Dear Amy,

Please, please help me. I am 12 years old and I go to St Helens Secondary School in Kings Cross. I am quite happy there, but there are these 3 girls that keep bullying me for money — and for fun. Every day I give them 25p each and I go without dinner. If I don't give them the money they get me in a corner and punch me in the stomach. I have quite a few bruises and I told my Mum and Dad. But they just think I'm lying and don't do anything about it. I don't really want to leave the school because of them. Please help. From bullied and depressed.

Dear Depressed,

Well, this is a very serious matter. If you haven't told your teacher already, I think you should. S/he could help you and the bullies will be sorted out. Talk to your Mum alone, and explain to her how you feel. Then she will understand. Tell her that this is affecting your school work and that you don't want to leave but it has to be sorted out. Tell her about the bruises. I hope this advice helps you very much.

Amy

Dear Mr and Mrs Cruge,

I've noticed that your son, Freddie, has been bullying certain pupils of our school. I'm extremely disappointed in your son, because he a very polite boy in normal circumstances. It is my duty to banish this pupil from our school for a period of time. He has been taking money off other pupils as well as bullying. Therefore, I ask you to come to discuss his welfare on 24th October 1989. If this is not possible, please contact the school on the above number. I do hope you co-operate.

Yours, E.G. Wright

Dear Mr Wright,

I received your letter and I'm truly sorry if Freddie has caused any trouble. The fact is that my husband drinks too much and gets in a state and then takes it out on Freddie by hitting him. Me too, if I butt in. Freddie is really a nice boy, but because his father is a violent man he thinks he can be violent as well. I have contacted social workers and Help Lines, but none have worked. I love my husband, but I think Freddie's confused because I am getting a divorce soon. Please give Freddie quite a bit of time off school so we can sort things out.

Yours sincerely, Jane Cruge

PS: The 24th October will be fine.

Girl who's afraid to go to school

G: Mum. I don't want to go to school.

M: Why not?

G: Because the girls are going to beat me up.

M: So what. You can beat them up.

G: No, Mum. I can't beat them up because they are bigger than me.

M: I thought they were in your class.

G: Ummm. Ummm. Yes they are.

M: Then why are you so scared of them. They are the same age as you.

G: Yes, but they are tough.

M: So why can't you be tough.

G: They know how to do karate, and stuff like that.

M: Right. I am going to teach you Karate. Now put your legs up and say Honga!

G: Honga Songo! Come on leg. Go up.

M: Right. You've got it in one love. Now go on. Bash them up.

G: Yes Mum. I am going to bash them up.

WHAT TO DO WITH MICHAEL TUCKER

Michael Tucker is someone we invented. We know he bullies other kids, steals their footballs and dinner money, picks fights, and causes a lot of trouble. If we are honest with ourselves we admit that we are scared of him. But what can we do?

I saw him once fighting over at the park, and he had a whole load of sand in his hand behind his back. When he came up to the boy to fight him he shoved it in his eyes...

When he is fighting all his mob's in a circle and he gets the person on the floor and they all start kicking him at the same time.

Let's talk to his friends and tell them not to be his friends. When he is lonely he might change his character. His friends are scared of him... They are just his friends so that they won't get beaten up.

If one person said he wouldn't pay money to him, then when he started picking on them they could get all their mates and just stand up to him.

Sometimes his friends are even worse than him. They are trying to imitate him, because they think he is a role model. They think he's really great and all that. Don't know why.

Maybe he is not as hard as he thinks he is when he is without his friends. Let's talk to his friends, and maybe we could confront him, or something like that, to stop him from doing what he is doing.

Maybe he is not like what he seems from the outside. On the inside he is probably different. Maybe we should all ignore him, so he will get the message.

I think he bullies because of how he is treated at home, and just to get respect from all the younger children. He does it to get friends. He thinks he wouldn't have friends if he wasn't hard. He thinks we would think that he was a wimp and wouldn't play with him.

Most of the time he does it after school and the teachers think it is not their problem.

I think it is the teachers problem if he is in school uniform.

Well just because he's outside of school they could still talk to him. They can help him with his problems. They could ask him to tell them what's going on at home, not exactly to say to him: You're picking on these kids and they're younger than you and all of that — because that wouldn't do much good. The way he's going on it's like he is big and mighty, but maybe the teachers just look at him on the outside.

If we gave him some help, like making him monitor for the books or chairs, and give him a role with power, give him something to do... he will get better and adapt and have friends, good friends.

If a few of us just start being good friends to him, and maybe show him that all of us do sometimes have the same problems as him, maybe he might think of us as good friends, and stop bullying.

HERE IS SOME ADVICE

In groups we discussed what advice we would give to new students about dealing with bullies. These are some of our suggestions. What do you think?

Don't play with bullies.

Ignore them.

Don't mix with gangs of bullies.

Don't give bullies money. If you give them money you encourage them to get money from you again and again.

Don't copy the way bullies act.

Don't let them push you around.

Stand up for yourself, even if you know you can't stand up to them.

Some bullies bully you because they know you are scared of them.

Some bullies bully because they are lonely, being ignored or under strain and in pain at home. They take it out on other children by bullying and taking money.

If they ask you for money, tell them that you have spent it... or just say NO! If ever, ever a bully uses violence on you, always go straight to a teacher. Get a teacher to help you.

Don't keep all of your feelings built up inside you. Make sure that you can talk to someone — like a close friend.

POSITIVE THINKING

It is not often we consider how special we are. There are so many things we can think and do. In our groups we looked at what we could all do: remembering how much we have in common. Then we looked at what some of us could do: finding out about our different abilities and skills. Finally, thinking very hard, each of us thought of something personal: discovering that each of us is different, individual, unique.

Everyone else is like no-one else

Everyone here can read, talk, drink, hit people, play, laugh, write, draw, touch, clap and blink our eyes.

Some of us can click our fingers, play the cello, play the guitar.

Some of us can spell, swim, play football, do voice impersonations, do gymnastics, speak a different language, eat pork.

But only I have a penfriend in Derbyshire; can go cross-eyed; can swim as well as this, and do these funny faces.

Only I can sleep in my bed, write with my pen, speak West Indian, speak a bit of German, do sign language, jump off quite a high roof, and wear my shoes.

I am weak I am strong Don't leave me on my own You are strong you are weak Don't keep it quiet: speak!

THE WORKSHOPS: AN ACCOUNT

1: The First Workshop

a) Preparation

Before this project I'd never done a workshop on bullying. I'd been teaching, for some of the time in secondary schools, for seven years. My subject was English and Drama. I also specialised in ESL/EFL, taught swimming and sport, and did my share of being Form Teacher and Tutor. Occasionally I came across incidents of bullying, and was shocked into action, but in all this time I never thought to do a workshop about it.

My position *was* one which I think is still common: leave well alone. If the class is functioning happily together, well and good if; there's a problem, sort out the 'bad apple' and hope. Bullying is abnormal, therefore it must be an isolated incident: bullying is a normal part of growing up in a cruel world, therefore there is not much you can do about it.

I share the English ability to assume that everything is going all right until it explodes. And the English capacity to be shocked by the explosion. A good example is the issue of child-abuse. Our increased awareness of the problem is won at the expense of the messengers who get blamed for 'causing' the explosion. Bullying, like child-abuse, is a 'can of worms' that people open at their peril.

Some people joked with me that I might encourage bullying by doing the workshops, and I respected their point. When Karen Smith, the Neti-Neti Administrator, was booking the tour of *Only Playing, Miss*, she found that many schools were aware of the need for action around the issue of bullying and saw the play as making a contribution to an already existing process. But not all.

With some of the enthusiastic schools it was question of finding the money. Teachers had to piece together the fee from separate funds, dip into the next month's budget, and even in some cases first find it from their own pockets! The tour was easily booked though, and indeed schools were soon queuing up for performances. *Only Playing, Miss* became part of a wider educational and media current of interest in the problem of bullying, and it was evident that Neti-Neti needed to further this by producing this book and the accompanying video, and by reviving the play for the schools who had missed it (or wanted it back). The play is disturbing: it shows cruelty as well as kindness, school with its harshness exposed. But honest art hurts for good reasons: real life just hurts. When I first read it, I thought back to my own school days and remembered the day a bully slashed my hand instead of the conker-string I was holding. In fact it is the hospital I remember most, the bully I've forgotten: he must have been a random thug rather than a personal enemy. Most painfully, I remembered the fights in the playground, in the corner under the horse-chestnut, which I hated myself for watching. I remembered the dilemma of standing there unable to avert my eyes, too scared to intervene, and knowing I should tell a teacher. I don't remember doing so.

Penny Casdagli and Caroline Griffin, the Co-Directors of Neti-Neti, seemed to have their own ideas about the structure and aims of the project, but left me a lot of (nerve-wracking) space to develop the content. The problem was that the content did not consist of a body of 'teachable' knowledge or skills, but of further smaller structures and aims. As I saw it, I had to reverse the normal approach of teaching (Why are you doing it? Who to? What are you doing? How?), and set up a learning process as if I were also a student: to make the workshops a process of self-education.

Apart from school and theatre, the only other workshops I had been involved in were in a men's self-help therapy group. Our emphasis was on talking about ourselves, although we did do some warm-ups and exercises. We tried to share rather than discuss, and to help each other talk about and practice doing things in new ways. I wanted to bring some of this experience into the bullying workshops, though with more emphasis on doing (acting, writing) than talking. I knew it would be difficult in large groups to get the intimacy needed for any 'therapy' work.

I decided that the workshops should explore all the roles involved in bullying as I remembered it from the playground: the bully, the victim, the bystander, the intervener, the teller. For each of these we could start with the question:
How does it feel? (personal experiences). And then ask:
What is it exactly? (teasing, exclusion, intimidation, assault etc.)
Who does it? (perceptions of behaviour, bullies, gangs)
Who is it done to? (those who are *and aren't* bullied)
Why does it happen?

Thus, having worked through the process, we would arrive at the teacher's starting point. I felt it was important that the children were not asked to be teachers, to have the answers. Jumping to conclusions would get nowhere: the children should be given the chance to explore their own behaviour and feelings.

In all I felt, as a teacher, that I had not done enough work in preventing bullying, that I myself had been reluctant to take incidents seriously, and that if this was the case with me it might be the same for other teachers.

I had read the literatur about bullying —see the Bibliography for details— but it inspired me more with awe than confidence. The phenomenon of bullying seemed to cover issues of size, gender, race, sexual orientation, disability, non-conformity, personal appearance, criminality, institutionalised violence, private crisis. I searched for an approach which could do justice to the seriousness of it without threatening the children with despair. I was not going to repeat the mistake of offering the violence and unfairness of the outside world as an excuse for not trying to make the class a safe and happy place.

The first thing to do was to talk to people. I asked all my friends about their schooldays. I listened to Caroline Parker, one of Neti-Neti's deaf actors, telling me what it was like to be at a school for deaf children. I phoned and visited teachers to find out who would be interested in having the workshops. In two cases I observed the class I was going to be working with. From my experience, I knew the problems involved in class work on sensitive and potentially violent topics. I would make sure I had small groups, precise roles, structured exercises, no premature focus on violent behaviour, and concentration on one mode of expression at a time.

I also had to consider my 'message' about bullying and how explicit I would make it. I hoped the message that emerged from the workshops would be not so much the responsibility of the victim to 'tell' someone they trust (as in cases of child abuse) as the responsibility of the whole class to take action whenever bullying was going on. And indeed for the whole school to do so. I firmly believe that anyone can become a victim if the bullies are powerful enough, but that bullies only become powerful in the absence of mutually supportive relationships (solidarity, friendship, 'good' authority).

I realised it was up to me to create a positive atmosphere in the workshops, to be the 'good' authority under whom the children could safely share and explore and pretend. I was worried that somebody in the group might be bullying or being victimised, and that this would narrow the focus on to personalities, giving status to the one or further victimising the other. I wanted the focus to be on the work of the workshop.

With all this in mind, I negotiated with teachers to set up three sessions with the same group of students. I asked for 12 to 15 in a group: in two schools I got 25. I wanted a Drama Room, or a classroom with flexible space — somewhere as private as possible. I needed enough chairs for a circle (or a carpet), and a few desks for writing tasks. I arranged to have pens, sugar paper and a few props. For some workshops I'd bring a little tape recorder or a video camera with me.

The workshops would last for about an hour. The teachers would either work with me (as team-teacher or participant), or take half the class into a separate room. They could then use the material I'd prepared, or just make the most of having half a class. The selection of groups would be made by the teacher in the light of my request for a multi-ability mix, averagely balanced in terms of race and gender and number of ESL-speakers. In the event I think interest in drama was also a factor.

Although I had experience of teaching in the multilingual classroom, I had none of working in schools for deaf children. The area of disability in education was not completely new to me, since I had spent a year teaching physically disabled children in Morocco. And I reckoned that if those polio-paralysed twelve-year-olds played football on crutches better than I could on two feet, then loss of hearing wasn't going to inhibit the students I'd now be working with. I also had the opportunity to learn a little sign language (British Sign Language or BSL — but in fact I always used Sign Supported English), which would alleviate some of my communication problems. I also knew I was going to be working with Caroline Parker (acting the teacher in the play) or Paula Garfield (Neti-Neti's Signing Advisor), both of whom had BSL as a first language.

What I was more worried about was avoiding being cut off by my lack of Bengali. The London schools I was to be working in, especially in Camden and the East End, had strong Bengali-speaking catchments, and I tried to think up strategies to adapt to this. Cath Cinnamon from the Central Foundation School for Girls shared with me her experience of enhancing the Bengali contribution to the English class, and I tried to devise exercises which would a) not exclude weak ESL-speakers, and b) be possible to do in Bengali (written or in dialect Sylheti).

With these factors in mind, I tried to think how I could use the tape recorder (in hearing schools) and video-camera (in both deaf and hearing schools) as a creative alternative to written work. I hoped they could become ways of doing things, as well as means of recording what was done. This got me thinking about what 'abilities' really are, my own included: I am an English language specialist, and a very verbal person, but I realised this itself could be a liability. And how many other 'abilities' are like this, I thought, solving one person's (communication) needs but at the same time creating problems for another?

I was reminded of this in my first week of working for Neti-Neti. I installed a phone extension into the office. As my diary says:

Though I say it myself, it looks a job well done, and I was only reminded of what I had already been acutely aware of in this all-female office — that here I was gaily filling the role of man about the house, when someone noticed my handiwork and, very jokingly, said it made her feel depressed. There is no joke without fire. One person's ability...

This reminded me to consider the effects of doing workshops in many different schools (single sex, mixed, multilingual, deaf) and with young people I didn't know: I would never be able to take my position for granted. I was not a teacher, not a guest speaker, not an entertainer. I most definitely was hearing, white, English-speaking, heterosexual and male. I am also bearded and six foot two, which was brought home to me when one boy said he couldn't imagine me ever being afraid — if he only knew! And I was working *with* the children in the exercises, giving my presence an impact beyond that of an instructor. By joining in I was also suggesting that childhood experience is something we grow up with, not out of. And that being hearing, English-speaking, white, male (and six foot two) exempts no-one from taking bullying seriously, whatever shape it takes. I knew I had to be scrupulously but implicitly anti-racist and anti-sexist in ensuring equal attention for each student. But I also needed to be far more aware than I had been of the assumptions my history and 'abilities' had given me.

b) Warming Up

I asked to be introduced as Francis, a writer with a theatre company, not Mr Gobey, a teacher. I suggested the workshops and play were not billed as being 'about bullying', which most teachers readily understood. It was good to meet a class in advance, even for a few minutes, but this was not always possible. In any case I still felt nervous: I had no idea how each new set of children would respond. It was like starting a new autumn term every day for a month.

Since time was short, I adopted the strategy of saying: Hello. I don't know you and you don't know me, but we'll get to know each other later. This is an acting workshop, and the first thing we need to do is warm up.

This, I found, was a better way of breaking the ice than one of those self-introduction memory games, which I hate. They knew each other's names anyway. I could learn them when they were working in pairs or groups. If we got straight down to 'work', it also headed off any challenging behaviour with which boys, especially, greet newcomers: Who are you? What famous actors do you know? and silently, What will you do if I fall off my chair/hit my neighbour/don't pay attention?

For the warm-up we always made a standing circle. I was in it, as were any other adults present. There were no bystanders: if we did 'silly' things there was no-one out there to judge and mock. We could all see each other and, although initially I led the 'games', I made sure that very soon others would get a chance to initiate ideas. These warm-ups were designed for use in schools with deaf as well as hearing pupils. The first game could be:

Chewing Gum

NB: in a circle, no props needed, no speaking.
AIMS: face and body warm-up
          individual to pair to group actions
Form a circle.
Focus on the actions.
Reaction sounds but no words.
You are chewing a piece of chewing gum. (No, not really.)
It is getting harder to chew. And bigger.
Chew enormously. Work those jaws.
Take it out.
Oh dear it's stuck. Shake it off. Throw it to somebody.
You are both stuck. Get help.
Throw it high into the air.
Catch it. Oh no. Stuck again. Shake, throw etc.
It lands in your/your neighbour's hair.
It is very big now. You are sinking under its weight.
Any solutions?
Blow a bubble. Slowly. Blow yourself up...
What happens?

This game is fairly elastic. You can stretch it in the middle with improvisations. One good group all stuck together. I was worried that it might get too boisterous, but as I grew in confidence during the workshops, I became more prepared to improvise *together*. But always within the understanding that violent behaviour is not allowed. My role is a leading one, but by example: I try to say as little as possible. I am interested in assessing the level of co-operation and acting confidence in the group, which can't happen if I hog the limelight. At least in a circle I don't need eyes in the back of my head. I do need eyes behind my eyes though, monitoring the group and the effects of my participation in it.

Incidentally this game has the benefit of being impossible to play if a pupil is really chewing, obviating the necessity for a workshop ban.

Another warm-up, which has many variations and is great fun, is the moving circle mime. This could follow straight on from 'Chewing Gum'.

Moving Circles

NB: explain as much as possible without speaking
                              choose one or two of the variations
AIMS: loosening of inhibitions
                              exploring body-language and mime
                              introduction to work on feelings

Leader initiates one of the following mimes.
And then passes on the leadership to someone else.

1) Imitation

Copy the way the person in front of you is walking. A sort of 'follow my leader' which can either lead to quite accurate mimicry or to increasingly grotesque forms of walking.

2) Hot and Cold

A leader mimes a type of ground (hot, cold, treacly etc). The others have to walk accordingly. Oohs and aahs can help sort out problematic terrains, but there should be no need for words.

3) Adverbs

A leader walks in a particular way (quickly, shyly, flashily etc). The others do their own version. The leader could set a useful example here by showing how to give the impression of walking very quickly without actually running.

4) Animals

Ditto, with and without sound effects.

I found it best to have the 'leader' jump into the middle and (especially in schools with deaf students) stamp their feet loudly.

Everybody freezes, the leader mimes, the circle follows and circulates in the opposite direction to before.

This reduces dizziness — unless you want to walk dizzily, that is.

While all this was going on I got to know the composition of the group, the dynamics, the 'characters', their level of inhibition, their willingness to open up in front of their classmates, their acting experience. And all of this would help me decide what to do next, and how quickly to move through the exercises. If, like the first group of third years I worked with, the pupils didn't hesitate before they leapt, I quickly moved the warm-up on to two areas I was interested in exploring:

Moving Circles 2

NB:	follows the above
	try to keep a rhythm going
AIMS:	expression of spontaneous feelings

Again the leader starts but soon passes the initiative on.

1) Emotions

Leader mimes the first feeling that comes to mind.

The others follow.

The feeling is expressed in the posture of the whole body, the walk, gestures and the face.

It is seen to build up and work through the body: sadness becomes tears, happiness becomes laughter.

2) Jobs you hate

Leader mimes being a sewage worker or doing the washing-up.

The others imitate.

3) People you like/hate

Leader may need to say who they are imitating since very few even famous people are recognisable by mime alone — my Madonna impersonation excepted.

In all cases I tried to keep the circle moving and freezing, setting up a rhythm where spontaneity is encouraged. I wanted to see what was on their minds, what feelings and images they had immediately available, because these would be useful later.

In fact mimes 2 and 3 did not work well the first time I tried them. I started with jobs, but found that in the framework of this game there was no time to develop convincing mimes. 'People you like' was better, with some exuberant imitations of Michael Jackson; 'people you hate' produced names of contemporaries. I decided to be more circumspect with this one in the future, without giving up my conviction that the workshops needed to deal with fear and loathing as much as love and trust. The mimes of feelings, though, became central to all subsequent first workshops. I found they worked exceptionally well with deaf pupils, who seemed more ready than most children of their age to release the physical side of strong feeling.

Having called out and mimed some emotions in the moving circle — whether as ways of walking, facial expressions, or angry monkeys — my next step was to focus on feelings. I wanted to use the release of energy which the warm-up had given to help locate the feelings. In the circle someone had jumped in the middle looking sad, and the group had felt the sadness through their faces and bodies. It was a question of feeling the emotion not thinking about it. Which is what happens in real life: you feel angry before you realise you are angry (unless you're a teacher... or an actor).

But now I wanted to do the realising part, and for this I arranged a brainstorm.

Feelings Brainstorm

NB: needs pens and large piece of paper
                    leader does not take part
AIMS: discovering and naming feelings
Place the paper on the floor.
Everyone kneels round it, pens poised.
You have 30 seconds to write down all the feelings you can think of.
Ready, go!

(It is possible to use a desk or the board, but it is more satisfying if everyone has to scramble together on the floor. If there are too many people for one piece of paper, use two — which adds an element of team competition)

At the end of a strict and dramatic 30 seconds, stop! They count up how many different feelings they've come up with. One person reads them out. Make sure everybody understands all the words.

If there was time at the end of the workshop they could add any feelings they had just remembered, but for the moment it became a finite list. I knew things were going well if no-one's immediate reaction had been to write 'bored'. The paper would be a mess of vivid scrawls, but I could decipher it later. They now had a few minutes to devise a mime in which the feeling they had chosen could be guessed at by the rest of us. (I too did not know their secrets, although I did go round with hints on body language, gesture, blocking, not corpsing etc.) I did have some role-cards up my sleeve, which I'd made for use with deaf children (with whom I learned to be extra-clear about setting up exercises), but I found them useful wherever a pair was having difficulties improvising:

Feelings Mimes

NB: preceded by Feelings Brainstorm
                    keep short and sharp
AIMS: to express and communicate feeling
                    to practice perceiving specific feelings
In pairs, with the odd three if necessary.
Each pair secretly chooses one of the feelings.
They prepare a mime centred on the feeling.

The mime can also tell a story, but the main purpose is to show the feeling.
Or feelings — alert pairs may show more than one.
Pairs should be encouraged to improvise their own situations.
Alternatively, the following role-cards can be used:

— *It is your first day at a new school. No-one speaks to you. At last someone asks your name.*

— *You have tooth-ache. You go to the dentist. The tooth-ache is cured.*

— *You are alone in a place you don't know. You meet a stranger.*

— *Your mother is having another baby. You go to visit. Your new sister screams at you.*

— *Someone grabs your bag. You go after them. They say they thought it was theirs.*

— *It's your birthday. Your best friend gives you a present. You don't like it.*

The stage is set and pairs perform their mime.
The audience has to recognise the feelings.

For the performances, the circle became a horse-shoe defining quite a small stage: running all over the place can be expressive of strong emotion but it doesn't communicate it. Perhaps I should have allowed interruptions, with the audience guessing aloud or putting hands up before the acting had finished — and this would have certainly abbreviated the saga of the snatched satchel in one girls' school — but I didn't want to discourage the performers. Nevertheless, I quickly learned to put a one-minute limit on the mimes.

Once the pair had performed, I asked them to stay 'on stage' and answer questions from the audience. First we had to recognise the feelings, then the situation. Usually someone was able to piece together the whole story. Often I didn't need to do more than commend a particularly skilful bit of miming, or lead the applause if others were reluctant. It may just be me, but I really like to make the most of even the smallest performance: introductions, respectful silence at the start, oohs and aahs during, wild applause, bows, the lot. I think it's brave to perform in front of your peers, so I feel making it an occasion can also emphasise the achievement. Especially for those, like ESL-speakers, for whom acting offers an unusual freedom.

The next step in this first workshop was to begin to focus more narrowly on behaviour. All being well, the students were now warmed up, enjoying themselves and primed to communicate/perceive feelings. I was not interested in acting skills as such, only in using the body as the centre for locating, realising and later reflecting upon common emotions. This was why I worked initially through drama and, more specifically, mime. All participants started from the same base, made the same effort to discover and communicate: there was no loading in favour of the articulate, everything had to work equally well for deaf and ESL pupils.

By this time I had a good idea of the pace the group could work at and, by weighing up the number of pairs/amount of reflection needed/time available, could judge which would be the best way to proceed. I also had to bear in mind my overriding aim of getting useful material recorded or written down. In my very first workshop the group did some excellent well-prepared mimes, including one sister/brother quarrel hilariously realised by two boys. These mimes were duly guessed and analysed by the audience, but at the end of it I grew anxious at having no record. Subsequently I concentrated on getting written work, but later, when I had 'enough', I again allowed more time to develop ideas.

The role-plays I continued with were one-to-one situations. They were still improvisations *before* the topic of 'bullying' had been introduced. It was important to find out what the students themselves came up with, also not to give too much weight to one type of behaviour. Again they worked on these pair role-plays in secret and then performed them to the rest of the group. Here are a few of them:

Role-plays

NB: see below for how to set up
                follows work on feelings

AIMS: to explore one-to-one situations and behaviour
                to find out what makes bullying behaviour

A teacher and a boy who has forgotten his homework for the third time.

A shy daughter owning up to her father that she has told him a lie.

A girl teasing a new boy who she thinks has funny hair.

An elder brother trying to get his younger sister to do his maths homework for him.

One girl trying to persuade another girl to join her in picking on someone in the class. She doesn't want to.

A strict teacher telling off a girl pupil for something she didn't do. The girl knows who did it, but won't tell.

A third-form boy getting a younger boy to give him money.

A brave girl out of school standing up to another, older girl who is teasing her about how she looks.

A girl and her younger brother fighting over who should have the comfy seat for watching TV.

A daughter telling her mother (or parents) that she is too afraid to go to school, because her classmates are ganging up against her.*

A boy making rude remarks in class to the clever girl sitting in front of him. She ignores him.

A girl calling her friend the worst names she can think of, just to see how far she can go.

A shy boy with a stammer trying to be friends with another boy who is in a bad mood. (Hearing schools only)

I tried these pair role-plays in various ways, choosing one of five following structures, which I explained carefully to the students:

Role-plays 2: The Five Variations

Continue with pairs from Feelings Mimes. (The role-play marked * can be done by a threesome.)

Give out role-cards randomly and in exaggerated secrecy. It is more acceptable in the long run for everyone to be subject to chance rather than to the prejudices of a dominant partner (or teacher).

If necessary explain beforehand that cross-gender acting is expected.

Set time limits on preparation (5-10 mins) and performance (1-2 mins).

Monitor each of the pairs during preparation.

Performances as with Feelings Mime.

Performers remain on stage while the audience guesses.

Audience must guess the characters, situation, story and feelings.

Conclude the whole session by making connections between the mimes.

1) Realistic short drama like you might see on Grange Hill.

Two-minute playlet complete with dialogue and props.
Needs lots of preparation.
Remembering dialogue is difficult.

This was good fun to act, and easy to understand. But maybe it was too easy for the audience: they recognised what was going on, but didn't really have to think about it.

2) Snapshots of key moments in the scene, like freeze-framing a video

Three frozen mime snapshots.
One performer announces the mime, they hold it for ten seconds, then unfreeze.
Keeping still was sometimes a problem.

This had the advantage of making the actors select very carefully the moment they wanted to show. They had to think about the relative status of the people, their expression, posture and gesture. In three snapshots they tried to tell the whole story. The audience had to work hard, and ask questions when they weren't sure. This was fun.

3) Miming the scene

Two-minute mime with minimum of props.
Establish each character first, before any interaction.

Miming is like putting lots of snapshots together. Without words the actors had to make pictures with their whole bodies. They had to work out appropriate ways of showing status, age, sex, and relationship with the other person. On top of this they had to show the situation and feelings. This was difficult, but the audience got very involved in working out what was going on.

4) Written scripts acted on to tape (only in hearing schools)

Each pair has one piece of paper.
After practising, they write their own dialogue in turn.

When the scene is finished they rehearse again, then perform to tape. This was a chance to write and to use dialogue and different voices to make characters. I recorded the scenes on tape, as in a radio play, and the participants were intrigued to listen to the sound of their voices as they pretended to be other people. These voices sounded strange but very powerful (mine did, too). By listening closely, the audience could interpret what was going on, and understand the feelings of those involved.

After the performance, when the group had identified the characters, the feelings and the story, I could ask: Who has the power in this situation? Who is behaving best? or Who is showing, who is hiding their feelings?

As you have seen, the role-plays are not all directly about bullying, but they have many features in common. In a perfect world there would be time to make connections, and the re-formed circle could pool their ideas about what everyone had just done: They're all about bullying. Teasing. One person behaving badly, one person being good. Being brave and strong. They're about friends helping you. It's all to do with power. Picking on people. Showing your feelings. Etc.

But usually by this time the pips were sounding and there were still two groups left to perform. My own sense of time is highly subjective, especially if I am enjoying myself. But I was loathe to eat into another teacher's period or the pupils' break: ideally I would arrange the workshop to end at a break, since I didn't have to rush away and there'd always be a few eager beavers wanting to replay the tape or just talk.

Sometimes I delayed a performance or two so that we could have time to reflect, but I found that the pairs who hadn't performed had forgotten or lost interest by the next workshop. Sometimes I finished off the acting and left the reflection, beginning the next time with a recap. But I preferred to start each new session with linked physical, oral and written exercises to give momentum to the proceedings. Sometimes I just left it, which was unfair on some of the students. All very unsatisfactory, but in many ways this first workshop was all a warm-up, and I could convince myself that it wasn't too bad if no writing had come out of it, or no fantastic insights into bullying. The main thing was that the students had started the process and enjoyed doing so. I hoped the seeds I'd planted would bear fruit in due course.

I said there were five ways I tried the role-plays. The final one introduced a new element. The dynamics of one-to-one situations are changed when a friend joins in, and I wanted to find a way of showing how this happens. With just two people, one older or stronger or in a higher position than the other, the relationship between them tends to be limited to the actions of one and the reactions of the other. A friend introduces another active force, and, by challenging the inequality of the relationship, brings it out into the open. And so in some later workshops I added the following variation:

5) Mime transformed by a friend

The situation is first mimed by the pair so that the audience can understand what is going on.
If there is any problem, freeze the mime and identify the characters.
Then, into the mime comes the friend, either a friend of the active or of the reactive character.
The friend tries to bring the drama to some sort of resolution.
The friend can also bring speech (or signing) into the mime.

In one example the friend (played by a mature and sensitive boy) persuaded the boy in a bad mood to accept the friendship of the boy with a stammer (played with doleful aplomb by a girl). This school had all hearing pupils so I set it up that the friend also brought speech into the mime. With deaf students the same effect can be achieved by having the friend bring sign language into a situation where only mime is being used. By speaking (or signing), the friend breaks the silence, and in so doing solves a problem.

I did this because one-to-one confrontations often end in silence (where their inequality has often begun). Even in everyday relations between parent and child, sister and brother, classmate and classmate, it is very common that a confrontation leads to the enforced silence of one of the parties: 'Shut up!/Be quiet!/I'm not talking to you./Go to your room!'. And I wanted afterwards to elicit the ingredients of bullying, one of which can be the infliction of silence, the denial of a right to reply.

c) Learning the Way

It was a Tuesday in the second week of my work. I had already done a few workshops and the materials, though not yet in the neatly rationalised state of the above summary, were there and working. Today I had two first workshops in schools I'd already been to visit. Both were co-educational, multiracial and in inner London.

The morning one inspired confidence. The first person I met was more than helpful — always a good sign — and politely asked a pupil to show me where to go — an even better sign. On the walls of the corridors were photos of sport and drama, self-portraits, artwork and colourfully painted notice boards. My contact teacher had prepared by selecting four students from four second-year English classes. The workshop got under way on time, and in an atmosphere of trust and excitement. I didn't finish everything in the plan, but was still very happy with the results. I had chosen to record the role-plays on tape, and now had at least some of them 'in the can'.

Full of my morning's 'success', I strolled into my afternoon school expecting to be able to produce the same committed rapport with another group of second years. After about thirty seconds I knew my programme wouldn't work. There was a lot of mistrust, hiding, running around, and hitting. I had to become a teacher, raise my voice, organise the most basic form of discipline. Whereas this morning's Feelings Brainstorm had garnered the whole range of emotions (with fear and guilt barely sneaking in), this one produced a short and depressing list — sad, miserable, under pressure, shaken up, happy. And the writing coming out of it was even more minimal than the mimes.

I was so angry: first with the children for 'misbehaving', secondly with myself for becoming the 'bad' authority. Even after talking about it, and going through my feelings of failure with the comfort of wise friends, I was kept awake that night by a phrase going round my head: There is another way. There is another way.

At the time I thought this referred to the 'system' and how it ought to be fostering safety, hope and learning in inner London. But on reflection I found there was a message in it for me: that my 'way' was essentially a way of working with people, not with material. Or to be more precise, each workshop would have its own way. And that doing dozens of workshops, honing my materials, refining my techniques and exercises, even writing this book — all of them would be a waste of time, if they failed to centre on specific groups and their individual members.

I had already made the basis of my work the premise that, although institutions could and should become more responsive and more responsible, each individual had to find their own way to deal with bullying. There was no single, teachable remedy. Also, that finding this way was a process of empathy and emotion, unique to each person. But what I hadn't done was to extend this philosophy to the level of my work in the workshops. I promised to do so.

2: The Second Workshop

a) The Research Project

It is difficult to describe the second workshop as it was quite different for each of the groups. In this chapter I relate what happened in the workshops in the two contrasting schools I've mentioned, and then give examples of other materials I used, and how and why I used them.

In the morning school, where I had the co-operation of the teacher and the trust of the children, I was able to combine finishing off the work of the first session with some group research and intensive personal writing. The finishing off consisted of putting the drama each pair had written on to tape, listening to them, and deciding what they were 'about'. I wanted to find out what each pair considered to be bullying, and what consensus there was among them. An experience in another school had alerted me to the dangers of premature class 'discussion': the circle was sharing personal experiences of being afraid and being picked on and one girl told of how she'd been teased. 'That's not bullying!' scoffed a big boy. And nobody contradicted him (or rather, I had to). This confirmed my preference for working with individuals, pairs and small groups before bringing the subject out into the general circle. I had been guilty of assuming consensus *before*, and it is a dangerous illusion.

The main part of the second session was devoted to group work, with a different research project for each group. I allowed no more than four to a group, and tempered the self-selection with a little persuasion. It was not that I didn't want single-sex groups, or only friends, or same language groupings — these are all supportive, potentially enabling, and certainly easier to organise. But I did want to promote an atmosphere of emotional daring. That sounds pretentious, but I do feel that everything you do in the classroom affects everything else, and that if you challenge pupils to take one sort of 'risk' (sitting with someone new, taking the fruits of one group to another), they are more likely to take other sorts of risk (telling the truth, admitting feelings of vulnerability). I am often more honest with strangers than with friends.

The projects were designed to provoke self-questioning and discussion, leading to a short piece of writing. Afterwards each group appointed a spokesperson to explain what research they had done and summarise the findings (in other schools I had these spokespeople rotate around the other groups).

I set it up as a *research project*, with much emphasis on the apparatus of enquiry: worksheets, questionnaires, statistics (3 out of 4 of us thought...), and formal interviews. One option on the sheets was for the students to interview each other, which I included as a mechanism to enable weak writers, ESL-speakers (and some others) to contribute fully. I made it clear that I expected each member to do their own thinking, research and (if appropriate) writing, then to share and discuss with the group, then to prepare what the group was going to tell the rest of the class. And I, of course, would collect in all their work, type it up on my computer, and bring it back to show them. In this case there was also the incentive that it might be included in Neti-Neti's book. I also explained that their work could, as in real social research, be anonymous. In fact few students this morning opted for that protection, but one boy wrote something he felt he could not share at all. But he kept it, which pleased me, as I've often done the same.

The first research topic was:

Feelings, Friends and Enemies

Feelings?

When was the last time you...
1) did something you were really proud of?
2) got very angry?
3) told the truth even though it was difficult?
4) hid what you really felt about something?
   (eg: pretended not to be jealous when you were)
Take one of these and write down the whole story.

Friends?

Which of the following statements about 'friends' do you agree with? A friend is...
1) someone I can be angry with and they don't stop being my friend.
2) someone who is always on my side, whatever I do.
3) someone who does what I say.
What do you think a friend is? Write down what you want your best friend to be like.

Enemies?

Which of the following statements about 'enemies' do you agree with?
An enemy is...

1) someone I don't feel bad about hurting.
2) someone I want to be friends with, who doesn't want to be friends with me.
3) someone who is different — not the same as me.

What do you think an enemy is? Have you ever had any enemies? Write down a short story about an enemy of yours.

This took up some of the ingredients of the first workshop's role-plays, and was designed to explore the value and costs of showing feelings, the give and take of friendship, and the nature of enmity. In fact it turned out to be too much, and in later workshops I divided the sheet into its component parts, and asked for more substantial pieces of writing. But of course I had to adapt to the age and abilities of the various groups, and with some asked for dramatic enactment rather than writing. The group doing this found a lot to talk about, especially over whether it was better for a friend to be loyal or honest, but they didn't write much, possibly because the slightly 'abstract' approach did not immediately lead into story-telling. See the Writings Section (p95).

The second worksheet was:

Who has power around here?

We all have power.
The power of our bodies.
The power of our minds.
And the power of our personality.

But other people have power over us.
Teachers, for instance, have some power over students. It is their job to use this power to help them learn.
Other people have power over us because we respect them, love them or fear them.
Think about your life.
Not just in this class, but outside too.
In the year. In the whole school. Among your friends. At home.
In each case answer the following questions:

1) Who has power over me?
2) What power do they have?
3) Do they use their power in a good way?
4) What power do they *not* have?
5) Look at Question 4 again. *Does* anybody have that power over you?

Feel your own power!
Your body. Your mind. Your personality.
Now write about your own power. Tell the story of how powerful you are.

The original idea behind this was in the questions I asked following the initial role-plays. It was during these that I tried to set the frame of reference for future work: I introduced the terms 'weak' and 'strong', but as categories of courage not of physique. I similarly introduced the word 'power' as a feeling of strength and a capacity to act. They are physical words, deeply embedded in our culture of discrimination against disabled people, but they are also figurative, and understandable as such by all users of language. This is because they are centred in the body, where our feelings make themselves known to us: I may be frightened, insecure or depressed, but what I feel is weak — my legs shake, my head swims, I find I can't lift a finger to help myself. Or I may be angry or in love, and feel very strong.

Working in sign language with deaf children helped me realise the slipperiness of spoken English. If you want to sign 'strong' in the figurative sense, you have to sign 'feel' first. But speaking too often fails to distinguish the two senses, and cultural images insist on their identity: a strong man cannot be weak. I wanted to get behind this right at the start to elude the collective fantasy that bullies must be big and strong. And I wanted to suggest that everyone has feelings of being strong and feelings of being weak (myself included). I didn't say this, but I tried in these opening stages of the workshops to imply that all of us share a capacity for behaving like bullies and their victims.

The above worksheet was meant to stimulate reflection on different aspects of power. Initially I wasn't specific enough and pupils got stuck once they'd written that teachers and parents had power over them (older boys tended to write 'my Dad' rather than 'my parents'). But with prompting, they were well able to trace the sorts of power people had over them, and make the transition to thinking about their own power.

The next topic in fact follows on from this, but there was no time for one group to do the worksheets in series. It is an attempt to be creative about the ups and downs of feelings by transforming them into song. *Only Playing, Miss* uses song in an integral and emotional way, both as an expression of a character's inner drama, and an active commenting chorus. I had wanted song-making in the workshops, but realised from past experience that it is very time-consuming, and only became a group activity in its final stages. This exercise was the preliminary to what should have been a longer process: in fact it turned out to be more like the research other groups were doing:

I am weak I am strong

You are going to make a song. You will write it together. It is about yourselves and your feelings.

Most songs are about feelings — love, jealousy, feeling all right. And yours is too.

Sometimes we feel good, confident, brave, happy...

In a word: STRONG.

Sometimes we feel bad, scared, miserable, lonely...

In a word: WEAK.

(Sometimes, perhaps, we feel both)

Each person is going to write two short verses.

The first one begins: *When...*
And ends: *I feel weak.*
And the second begins: *When...*
And ends: *I feel strong.*
The song can rhyme if you want it to, but it doesn't have to.
It can also be set to a tune that you know.

Here is an example:

When I write my best
and teacher says
'You must write it out again
in neat!'
It's times like this I feel weak.

When I'm with my friends,
they share with me
everything they think is
going on.
It's times like this I feel strong.

When you have written your own two verses, join them up with the others.
Write down the complete song.

The other worksheet that I used that morning was the one most directly concerned with bullying. It was important because it led on to the rest of the workshop and in to the decision-making exercises I had planned for the third session. It took the form of a questionnaire with several yes/no questions followed by a call for a more detailed response to one of them. In the group the students worked in pairs asking each other the questions, and then wrote out a story from their own experience:

Have you ever..?

Think carefully before you answer these questions.
When you first read through, just answer yes or no.

Have you ever...
1) sided with a group which was picking on someone?
2) sided with someone who was being picked on by a group?
3) teased someone younger than you, again and again?
4) answered back at someone who was teasing you?
5) used force to get your own way?
6) stopped being friends with someone because nobody else was friends with them.
7) started being friends with someone unpopular?
8) sent someone to Coventry? i.e. 'blanked' someone by not talking with them?

Now choose the question you found most interesting.
Write down as much as you can remember of your own story.

If you want you can do this worksheet with a partner, asking questions, choosing the most interesting, asking more about it, and then writing down as much as you can find out of your partner's story.

This proved to be the most productive topic in terms of the amount written. Everyone had a story to tell, often about their time in Primary School, although one pupil told of an incident that had happened the week before when he had intervened on behalf of someone being teased. This, and other examples are to be found in the Writings Section (p95). When I discussed this questionnaire with a teacher at another school, she said she wouldn't expect many yeses for question 2, and in fact it surprised me that there were so many. It was questions 7 and 8 which got fewest yeses, and no writing. A couple of times I had to explain what sending to Coventry means: a good sign that it's an obsolescent usage, but no guarantee that ostracism no longer goes on.

In schools for deaf children, I felt better use could be made of the workshops if I concentrated on acting so I passed the research project side over to my contact teachers. They found that these worksheets worked best if they were simplified and dramatised. I was amazed when one of them told me he had spent a whole lesson on the Have you ever..? topic, and that the pupils had had 'great fun' with the concept of sending to Coventry. They knew very well what exclusion from a group entailed, but not this way of 'saying' it.

The afternoon session did not this time try to imitate the morning. Part of me dreaded going back. I had asked for a room with a video and monitor in it, hoping that the smaller room would also help foster a group spirit. I had also requested the support of one of the two drama teachers, and got it. The video I was going to show was a clip from Neti-Neti's signed story-telling of the previous year made during rehearsals for *Beggar In The Palace*, (which, like *Only Playing, Miss*, was also performed in Bengali, Sign and English).

The story was of Odysseus and the Cyclops. One of the boys (who crowded the front row, leaving the girls at the back) knew a little of the story, another had seen sign-language, but I decided anyway to play the clip twice: first with speech, then with signing alone. If the story had been universally known I might have risked skipping the spoken narrative altogether, but as it was the group had to 'read' the signs, say what was happening, and thus reconstruct the story. Then in pairs they tried telling bits of the story to each other in sign-language. I was around to help, but tried to use only sign-language myself.

The main aim of doing this was to prepare for the play by opening up a new area of communicative possibility. I wanted to show how expressive signing can be, and how exciting for hearing pupils to try to understand and use. Not that easy, but at least possible. The other aim was to provide a special, new and challenging activity for this particular group, to try to get them working more together, and more constructively.

After that I planned to show a short extract from a TV drama to stimulate 'What do you think happens next?' discussions and role-plays. But as it turned out, the video clip refused to work at normal speed so I had to change plan. I hate it when technical things go wrong in the middle of a class. My own mistakes with pause buttons and lens caps I have learnt to laugh off — in fact I think I use my own incompetence as a teaching aid — but machines going wrong on their own make me feel stupid. I become panicky and unable to think constructively. In this case I abandoned the video and reverted to the group research worksheets. The ones I chose were Have you ever..? and Feelings, Friends and Enemies, as they seemed likely to be the most successful. In addition to writing, each pair or group had the option of calling me over with my tape to record their stories.

Once the class settled down, this more or less worked. The presence of the teacher was very helpful here, since recording precludes general class supervision, and the more vulnerable members of the class were able to feel safe in the teacher's company. In fact by now I had seen that last week's rowdiness was really only coming from one disturbed boy, and took pains to give him a lot of attention. Unfortunately this reduced my availability to other groups, especially one group of girls doing the exercise in Bengali, which I was keen to tape.

It was more in this school than anywhere else that I was forced to reassess my role in the workshop. I have said already that I had to become more like a teacher, wielding more authority than elsewhere. I also could no longer go about the work without regard to race or gender, treating everyone as equal participant; I had to become a positive discriminator.

With more experience I would have found a way to end this workshop with the group working together, but at this stage I wasn't confident enough in sign language to make it the shared new medium for communication. As it was, the Bengali-speaking girls kept themselves to themselves, the one mother-tongue English-speaking girl sat on her own, and there was no interaction with the boys — who didn't appear to want it either. The individual taped stories were very revealing, but they didn't feel right for ending up on. So I tried to bring the session to a close with a poem. Here it is:

Back in the Playground Blues

Dreamed I was in a school playground, I was about four feet high
Yes dreamed I was back in the playground, and standing about four feet high
The playground was three miles long, and the playground was five miles wide

It was broken black tarmac with a high fence all around
Broken black dusty tarmac with a high fence running all around
And it had a special name to it, they called it The Killing Ground.

Got a mother and a father, they're a thousand miles away
The Rulers of the Killing Ground are coming out to play
Everyone thinking: Who they going to play with today?

> *You get it for being Jewish*
> *Get it for being black*
> *Get it for being chicken*
> *Get it for fighting back*
> *You get it for being big and fat*
> *Get it for being small*
> *O those who get get it and get it*
> *For any damn thing at all*

Sometimes they take a beetle, tear off its six legs one by one
Beetle on its black back rocking in the lunchtime sun
But a beetle can't beg for mercy, a beetle's not half the fun

Heard a deep voice talking, it had that iceberg sound:
'It prepares them for Life' — but I have never found
Any place in my life that's worse than The Killing Ground.

Adrian Mitchell

(from M. Rosen. Kingfisher Press, 1985)

Previously, where there had been more time, it had provided opportunities for language, mime and sign work. Each group took on a verse and performed it in their own way, and then it was put together as a finished piece. I saw it as a First Act closer: a blues number which begins in sadness at the remembered misery of being bullied, but ends in anger at the irresponsibility of adults who allow bullying to happen. For me it represented a moment of realisation in the 'journey' of the workshops, the moment when the play becomes serious, when something you've been going along with for a long time suddenly becomes horrible. The workshops so far had been mostly play — warm-up games, acting, role-playing, story-telling — but now I wanted to suggest the seriousness of it all.

I found the poem shocking, especially since I had just been made sensitive to so many similar experiences and and feelings, and I took no comfort from the last verse. But the mere performance of it sends two important messages: my reading of it says *Here is one person who does take the playground seriously;* the children's own performance of it says *We are angry at what is happening; it's really bad, what can we do?* Coming at the end of the second workshop, the poem marks the transition from negative to positive, from not coping to coping, from keeping to oneself to sharing with others. And it is a process that everyone has gone through, even if they were unaware of it. This afternoon the process faltered, and only the first half of the poem's message was transmitted, but I left looking forward to the next workshop — which was something.

b) Getting in Touch

In each school the workshops took a different route on the same journey. Different for two reasons: one, I made them so by experimenting with different materials; and two, the pupils themselves helped find their own route (which I had to be sensitive to). The point of doing a workshop, or rather a series of workshops, was to deepen the responses by getting the children doing 'work' on themselves, individually and as a group. *They* were the subject of the workshops, not the abstract issue, 'bullying'.

What happens all too often with sensitive topics, when they are not ignored altogether, is that they get split off into the realm of speculation. They become something to talk 'about'. Try this exercise on yourself:

Hypotheticals?

Consider this statement.
1) 'I would feel angry.'
Try saying it in different voices.
Does the meaning change? How close are you to the feeling?
How involved are you in making the statement?
Now say:
2) 'I feel angry.'
Whisper it. Shout it. Raise your eyebrows. Rage. Smile.
Ask yourself the same questions.

Can you hear how the present indicative expresses the emotion, the body of emotions, whilst the subjunctive distances it to the armchair of probability?

It is no good expecting to engage strong feelings in hypothetical situations. If you want solutions based on detached reasoning, that's fine, but those solutions will bear little relation to what is actually done in heart and soul crises.

Abstract reasoning 'about bullying', especially at the level of new entrants into secondary school, was unlikely to offer really strong connections with the nitty gritty of everyday school life. Asked what they would do if confronted by a bully, most children say: 'I wouldn't be scared', 'I'd punch him' or 'I'd get my big sister'. And it is important for their own self-respect that they say this. They agree that bullying is wrong, that victims should stand up for themselves, and that bullies should be punished, but the price they pay for this emotional and moral certainty — which adults share — is that they have fended off recognising the real nature of their own conduct (as well as their own part in the dynamics of group behaviour).

For this reason 'What would you do if..?' questions played no part in the 'work' of the workshops. Once the 'work' was done, the feelings found and engaged, the roles enacted and reflected on, the personal dilemmas worked through, the social behaviour practised and understood, then it became possible to hypothesize.

And in the same way it was only then, after the 'work', that it would become possible to *discuss* the problem. Consider this:
'The worst thing you can do with a problem is discuss it.'
Discussion is so often promoted as the first step in dealing with an issue, when it is in fact the last thing you are able to do.

It comes at the *end* of a long process of discovery, self-liberation and learning.

Discussion assumes:
1) articulacy
2) an approach to the issue in the abstract
3) the participants' freedom to speak about it
4) their willingness to communicate with each other

None of these is readily available to the victim, nor to the perpetrator of the abuse.

Both have a long path to travel before they are free enough from their own history to discuss it.

My diary notes:
'Being able to discuss something is itself a freedom: the something is already able to be discussed, and discussing it wont make you any more free. If you are not able to discuss something (ie: it's too deeply involved with your lack of freedom), then discussing it could actually make it worse.

It could not only divert you from looking inwards, but even oppress you with a sense that *only you* are so deeply unfree in this way.

I'll make this the watchword of the workshops, even if it seems they are operating on a childish level of playing rather than 'analysing'. For that is where the pearls and daggers are.'

The workshops were about making connections. Connections between the formal discipline of school life and the informal behaviour of children outside adult supervision. Between what is taught in class and what is learnt in the playground. Between what they think when they are on their own and what they say in front of their friends. We could 'play' all of these and experience in them in a safe made-up way.

Here is a game I first used with deaf students:

The Unhappiness Game

NB: needs some experience of mime and sign to work
needs to be demonstrated simply and clearly

AIMS: to open up area of feeling vulnerable
to sidestep inhibitions about sharing this feeling

Get in groups of 3 (or 4).
One of you is unhappy. It is a secret unhappiness.

The unhappy one writes the reason for their unhappiness on a slip of paper. Then goes back to the group.

The group has to find out what's wrong.

They can mime guesses (being told off, beaten up etc).

Or they can proceed by a sort of twenty questions logical deduction: first of all finding out whether the cause of the unhappiness is at home, school, between friends, members of family etc, and gradually arriving at the real reason.

The unhappy person can only nod or shake their head (more or less enthusiastically).

Their unhappiness is a secret — but they want it discovered as well.

(The next player might choose a more obscure reason for their unhappiness, but the miming and logic of the group will improve to make 'getting through' easier.)

If one group finishes — all its members having taken a turn — they can go and help another group. The class will then finish the final discovery together.

(But, as with most games: if it drags, clues may be given. The unhappy person is allowed to help the group if they are 'warm'.)

This is rather a complex game to set up, and the first time I tried it, my explanation (via sign language) was not clear enough: the unhappy person wanted to take the initiative. This was natural, since there are not many games where the group initiates a tender enquiry into the hurt feelings of an individual — groups usually oust misfit players and their 'serious' feelings. But the point of the game was to find out the cause of an unhappiness the individual was *not* keen to communicate: it was up to the group to find a way of 'getting through'. Perhaps the 'unhappy' player was in too difficult a position: on the one hand pulling a long face and pretending to be unhappy because their dog had died; on the other gleeful at their power in the guessing game.

I tried to get around this difficulty by:
a)   having each player write down their reason for unhappiness — so they couldn't change their mind midway
b)   supervising the initial stages
c)   emphasising that each player has a go at being unhappy and being a member of the miming group and in a subsequent workshop:
d)   introducing 'moulding' mimes (see below)

In addition to this I wanted to round off the game with something which would bring together the whole class. The first time I played this game I had the participants symbolically shred the 'unhappy' slips of paper, but this felt dishonest — secret negative emotions do not just disappear when you share them — so I never did it again.

The Unhappiness Game: Conclusion

The 'unhappy' slips of paper can now be used.

Each group of 4 picks one of the causes of unhappiness they have correctly guessed and mimes the whole story together.

They mime *both* the original event *and* the story of how they found out what the matter was.

Thus the rest of the class can share in the sorrow and the success of a supportive intervention by friends.

Each mime acts out the adage: a sorrow shared is a sorrow halved.

With deaf children who use sign, this particular game became a bit static: there was little incentive to mime when the same information could be conveyed more efficiently by sign. I saw this, but at first thought it would be unfair to ban signing altogether. I should have had more courage, because at the heart of the game lies the notion of communicating in a language you are not fluent in. Getting through so that someone understands how you are feeling is a challenge in any language, but strangely it is sometimes easier when your first language is denied you. With hearing children the game had this additional element of challenge: they could become so involved in 'getting through', in the limited and unfamiliar medium of mime (or sign), that they might lose some of the inhibitions they had about saying difficult things.

Hearing adults know this. You can say things on the phone you'd hesitate to say face to face, and if the line is crackly you make your meaning even clearer. You can shout things in someone's ear at a disco you'd be embarrassed to repeat in the street.

But it is a two way process. The 'interference' also challenges the listener to greater participation. Her misunderstandings, questions, sympathy, interpretations and impatience add to the urgency of 'getting through', and make the achievement mutual.

This is my rationale behind many of the workshop exercises. By concentrating on ways of communicating — mime, sign language, languages other than English — and in each game using just one medium — voices on tape, facial expressions on video, letters, phone calls, angel voices — I emphasise the common purpose of all languages, which is also the purpose of the game: making contact. And beneath this lies the intuition that making contact with other people and making contact with one's own feelings, are two sides of the same coin.

I mentioned earlier a variation of The Unhappiness Game that involved 'moulding' mimes. Moulding is when one or more active players moves a passive player into a particular shape. It is like a frozen mime, except that the moulded player is not 'expressing' some action or emotion, but having it 'impressed' (gently) upon them. As you can imagine, this requires a high degree of co-operation and trust among the players, since it can also be an opportunity for malevolent manipulation. I set it up gradually by means of linked warm-up exercises:

Squeezes

NB: Probably not suitable for large groups

AIM: Fun. Trust. Togetherness. Introducing 'moulding'.
    All stand in a circle.

Hold hands and close eyes.

(If this proves difficult, one adult can stay outside the circle as a figure of safety.)

The group leader explains the rules:

Eyes closed at all times.

No speaking. Do exactly what is done to you.

The leader sends a right-hand squeeze around the circle.

Each player passes it on.

The squeeze remains the same.

When the squeeze has returned, the leader sends a different one (perhaps finger and thumb only). This time the squeeze should circulate faster.

Complications can be introduced: a faster tempo, a left-hand squeeze circulating in the opposite direction, other players taking the lead, multiple squeezes.

The whole thing will probably collapse in laughter.

When I was the only adult present I chose to be 'in touch' with the children and lead as a participant, and I didn't open my eyes — promise! Of course I was tempted to, but that was the rule. As a result the game took longer to settle down, and I'm not sure what happened to some of the squeezes. In fact the first time I played it I didn't have the players holding hands, but passing on 'moulding' movements. This, I soon realised, was stage two: it needed a build-up of trust to succeed — if your neighbour is out of touch with you, you are vulnerable; if you are already holding hands it feels safer.

Safer, but still a risk. I could hear which of the players opened their eyes, and it was often children who were unwilling to take other risks in the workshop. But the more successful this game was in establishing an ethos of trust — it's okay to hold hands, even of a boy/girl, okay to close eyes, anti-social to break the rules or to use force — the more successful was the rest of the workshop.

You can't enforce trust, but if there is another adult present, they can remain outside the circle and ensure that the rules are followed — which at least gives trust a good name.

Moulding Circle

NB: to be played after another touch warm-up (see above)
AIMS: development of touch awareness.
        All stand in a tight circle, shoulder to shoulder. Relax.

The group leader explains the rules:

Eyes closed at all times.

No speaking.

Do exactly what is done to you.

The leader turns to their right-hand neighbour and makes a simple moulding movement eg: crosses their arms.

This player, having felt the moulding done to them, passes it on around the circle.

To avoid impatience, the leader must chose a simple movement to start with, and follow it up with a more complex one. If there is an outside person they can contribute to the game by silently 'moulding' a new leader — which can also be surprising for the old leader!
A good way of finishing the exercise, and returning to the 'real' world, is for each player to drop out of the circle after they have completed the moulding of their neighbour.

They can then open their eyes and silently watch the rest of the game, noticing how different the movement looks from the outside.

In this game each player knows who touched them. I could, I suppose, have formed a random circle by means of another game, but that seemed excessively complicated. Both games practise communication by touch and build up an awareness of touch quality. I kick myself now for not thinking to play these games with deaf children — perhaps I baulked at the idea of depriving them of another sense. Because deaf children are virtuosi of touch: virtually every communication is preceded by a touch, signalling presence and attracting attention. It was a salutary lesson, learnt in a school for deaf children, that raising my voice was no good: the inattentive student must be reawakened by a wave or a touch. And it was deaf students who were least inhibited in expressing the physical side of feelings — laughing, crying, jumping for joy — and most intricate in their chewing gum knots. I expect they'd love this touch stuff.

There was another game, which Gillian Emmett, a teacher and former ILEA Drama Advisor, showed me, which tested a player's ability to recognise a particular person's touch. I'll call it:

Who touched me?

NB: works best if players can't anticipate
AIMS: a quiet warm-up; touch awareness; trust.
Players are divided into 'A's and 'B's.
The workshop leader stays out of the game and directs it step by step.
There is no speaking.
'A's sit on the floor and 'B's stand beside them.
'A's close their eyes.
'B's move to a different partner and mould them with a simple movement.
'B's retire to the edge of the acting area.
'A's open their eyes, get up, and go and stand beside the person they think moved them. The 'B's nod or shake their head.

Here the leader can break the silence by asking:
How do you know who touched you?
(It surprised me how many got it right.)
The game can repeated vice versa, but it should not become too complex.

All these games are really preparations for using the technique of moulding in work more directly related to the bullying theme. Penny Casdagli told me she had used it in a workshop with drama students: groups had moulded 'bullies' and 'victims' out of passive bodies. I didn't do this exactly, but I did introduce a moulding element into the Unhappiness Game and some of the role-plays.

The Unhappiness Game: Moulding

NB: this is an alternative, not a sequel to the original game
AIMS: communicating through touch
        exploring individual and group pressures

In this variation the unhappy player is no longer a nodding spectator.

She returns to the group, having written down the reason for her unhappiness.

She then shows them how she is feeling by moulding their bodies into an unhappy pose.

The group makes a guess at what the situation is (in sign or speech). More mime mouldings might be needed to identify the precise cause. (For instance, it might be a particular schoolbook that has been lost.)

Once this is done, it is the group's turn to mould the unhappy player. They bring her into the mime.

They mould her into a new freeze, illustrating a possible course of action.

(For instance, explaining the loss to a sympathetic parent.)

If this is successful they finish by moulding her into a happy pose.

Everyone ends up happy.

Selected mimes are performed to the whole class, interpreted, and reflected upon.

I think it is important that this version of the game operates this way round: the individual communicates a feeling of unhappiness to the group, and then the group — once they have fully understood the unhappiness — supports the individual with comfort and ideas. It is, unfortunately, the opposite of what often happens in real life, where groups are experienced more as 'pressure' than support. When you consider that sharing a feeling with someone offers a joy like no other, the neglect of rewarding this behaviour at school becomes very strange. As a baby I chortled and was played with, cried and got cuddled, but in school there were no prizes for being happy, no extra attention for being sad. I soon learnt to hide my feelings, first from the teachers, who didn't seem to care about them much, then from my groups and gangs, who demanded sociability, and finally from myself. Being able to cope became the key to school success, and any sign of not coping smelled of failure. But none of us can cope on our own, no child, no adult. We all need support. Sometimes we need it desperately.

One purpose of this game, then, was to offer an balanced example of positive group/individual relations: the individual moulds the group, the group moulds the individual. It never occurred to me to play the game with another emotion, joy for example, as there wasn't the same inhibition about communicating it, about impressing it on others. Also, being unhappy is an obvious consequence of being bullied, as is a reluctance to tell anyone; and by now many pupils were choosing bullying as a theme.

In fact I'd set it up with the bullying situation in mind, as I wanted an exercise which combined communication of feelings and communication between an individual and a group. This exercise was both very intimate — one person moving another's body — and quite social — three or four people working together. And the images that resulted in the freeze mimes, postures, gestures and faces had the advantage that they were shared: in acting terms they didn't demand the expression of a (faked) emotion, but the bodily acceptance of someone else's.

And this is the aim behind the exercise. The children are practising the most basic means of communication, the one as adults they will increasingly ignore, but which is the root of human interaction, and the root of much of our language about it: touch, be in touch with, be touched, be moved, be impressed, communicate, get together, connect. I have already said how I try to locate emotions in the body as a first step to experiencing them fully. It is the same here: to be moved (physically) can be a realisation of what it feels like to be moved (emotionally).

It can also be very labour-intensive on the part of the group leader. Children giggle, flop out of role, get shy, break the rules, seize the chance to be sly, and get bored even when you are doing the most amazingly interesting things. It is necessary to spend time building up 'seriousness' and trust, which is one of the reasons I made a point of taking part myself, and as the professional leader of an 'acting workshop' (although different exercises gave me different roles). I found it helpful to warm up energetically, move quickly between exercises, and link one session's work so that common threads could be drawn out at the end. I tried to balance each session (and each exercise if possible) so that it started in *engagement*, with everyone bound up in the game, moved through a stage of *expression*, where each player could develop their own way, and ended in a short period of *reflection*.

Of course it didn't work smoothly, and several times I had to stop an exercise to explain it again or to abandon it and go on to something else. I learnt to be more flexible and to trust my instinct about how things were going. I never really finished a workshop though. I had three in each school and wished I had four, but I'd probably have run out of time just the same.

c) Turning Points

1: 'Listening' and 'Talking'

It so happened that I had not read the script of *Only Playing, Miss* before preparing much of my material for the workshops. Nor had I seen it in performance. The Neti-Neti acting version of the script was ready in mid-September and rehearsals began in mid-October, but I'd been doing workshops from the start of the September term.

This was very useful in practical terms, since I was able to pass on to the actors what I learned in the schools. I showed them the materials I'd used and much of the writing the children had already done, which they said they found helpful. But at the time of the workshops I had no idea what effect the play would have: I was convinced it was good, however, and I was committed to Neti-Neti's integrated approach. I had enjoyed *Beggar In The Palace* — a multilingual drama about Penelope and Odysseus — and could appreciate how schools had found its linked themes of marriage, recognition, multicultural myth and multilingual communication, an intriguing source of follow-up work. Would the theme of bullying be so accessible?

In an obvious sense *Only Playing, Miss* was 'about' bullying, but I now realised that there was a common ground beneath its other themes of friendship, hiding and showing strong feelings, and behaving under stress. And this was also communication: as an inner process of awareness and an outer process of interaction. The three languages used in performance would serve to emphasise this further. I wrote in my diary:

> What is a bully? Isn't a bully someone who fails to communicate with their own inner feelings but 'recognises' them in someone else? Aren't they desperate to get through to their chosen victim — someone vulnerable, but visibly so, unlike themselves — to uncover feelings of vulnerability they repress? And is it anger at their own inability to communicate, except by causing pain, which fuels this fixation?

> The important thing is communication: it is at the very centre of *Only Playing, Miss* — the play, the workshops, and the issue of bullying itself.

This was confirmed for me later at The First National Conference on Bullying, organised by Kidscape (see Index) in October 1989. Every speaker had something to say about the importance of communication: among children, between children and teachers, among adults. One noted that if professionals fail to understand their own feelings, they fail to understand others'; and they then fall into the common institutional trap of blaming the victim (or of blaming the bully). Researchers showed profiles of characteristics of bullies and victims, and offered statistics (eg: 20% pupils at some time afraid to go to school, only 48% neither a bully nor a victim, only 33% of bullies not themselves bullied) which had me reeling. So many incidents of bullying not seen, so many cases of long-term damage (to bullies as well as victims), so many children not being listened to.

But listening was one of my main roles in the workshops. Soon after starting, I realised that a crucial moment of the 'journey' would be when we all sat around in a circle and listened to each other. I had thought this might be near the beginning, a sort of launch-pad for other exercises, but the more 'work' had preceded it, the better it turned out. This is because talking from the heart is very, very difficult. I knew this already, and I prided myself on being a good listener (if not such a good talker). It took the new experience of working in a school for deaf children to make me reassess what I meant by 'talking' and 'listening'. I found it extraordinarily difficult to relate to deaf children as a group, even when there were only nine of them. Suddenly all my skills seemed verbal. I saw what an incredibly complex bit of communication a ten-way 'discussion' really is.

And when Paula Garfield, Neti-Neti's profoundly deaf Signing Advisor, conducted a signed circle-talk about bullies, the shifting focus was too much for some of the participants, and they shut off completely — I saw signs of that 'overload' Caroline Parker had warned me was likely. In fact I saw all the little breakdowns that happen in a hearing situation, but at five times the speed. It renewed my respect for the teachers at that school, but decided me on simpler structures for the future.

Returning to hearing schools, I understood that the circle-talk needed more preparation. Especially if the 'talking' was going to approach 'being honest', and 'listening' was going to become 'empathising', which I had decided were the full figurative meanings behind those able words. The group needed practice in working together, working on their own experiences and feelings, and tuning in to other peoples'. I also felt that this particular exercise would be less accessible for second language speakers, and didn't want to appear to exclude them at the outset. These considerations pushed the circle-talk to the second or third workshop.

But there was another problem bothering me: how to set up the circle-talk, which I imagined as a free-flowing therapeutic exchange of stories and suggestions. I didn't want a class discussion 'about' bullying in the abstract; I didn't want identification of a particular member of the group as a bully or a victim of bullying. It was Gillian Emmett who suggested the solution of having an empty chair and an imaginary bully. What a good example of making a 'drama' out of a crisis!

In this exercise I took part in the circle and asked leading questions. This is why I use the pronoun we. As the talk developed I needed to say less and less.

The Bully Circle

NB: needs preparatory work and good class trust

AIMS: to share experiences of being in a situation where bullying was going on

       to achieve some consensus and realise the power of the group

We sit in a tight circle of chairs.

One of them is empty. In it sits the class bully.

Not a real person, but real enough to keep our eyes on.

I ask:

> What is this bully like?
> What sex?
> What size?
> What appearance?

Each question is an opportunity for the children (and me) to voice an experience of a real bully.

I use the empty chair to bring us back to talking about this one imaginary person.

Each decision is made on a rough consensus.

Next I ask for stories of what this bully has done, not in general but to each one personally:

> What happened?
> How did you feel/react?
> What happened next?

At this stage the bully seems to be growing, so I ask:

> Why are we afraid?
> How come s/he's so powerful?

And, if no-one else does, I direct attention to the bully's position in *this* class (not the fifth form or a comic strip):

> Does s/he have friends?
> What are they like?

They have to begin to take responsibility for the bully as a member of the class, and someone they can do something about.

But what can we do to solve our problem?

Is there also a way (maybe it is the same way?) of solving the bully's problem?

Because by now it is obvious that the bully's behaviour is not doing them any good either.

And, as they discuss strategies, someone asks:

Is this problem too tricky to solve on our own?

Can we get help from a teacher or parent?

This exercise was a dramatisation of the power of bullies. It was not about victims. This tied in with my conviction that the workshops had to look squarely at bullies, not get bogged down in what makes a victim. It is obvious what makes a victim: a bully. Bullies are the problem, victims are the result of bullies' problems.

Imagining the bully was a way to talk about someone's characteristics and behaviour without implicating anyone in particular. There was still some danger though. In one circle (1st year girls):

One girl took a remark about goofy teeth personally and to heart. Good example of the way a group can intimidate and 'victimise' unintentionally — or perhaps someone's dig slipped into the game. But group judgement creates both bullies and victims, even if it is up to the latter as to whether they are susceptible to the roles created for them.

If the group is not used to working together or if one person's fantasy tends to dominate, it can be difficult to focus sufficiently to conjure up the empty chair bully, which is why you can't do the exercise 'cold'. The difficulty is important though: it is not that each person cannot see a figure in the chair, but that the figure is not the same for everyone. They are not used to sharing their fears, or recognising those of their classmates: one says the bully is big and ugly and loud-mouthed, another insists she is small and sweet and sly. Both are monsters fashioned out of intimidation and private fear. After one (mixed, multiracial, 2nd year) circle, I noted in my diary:

Sitting in the empty chair was the bully, Michael Tucker: blonde, big, spotty, hefty. His presence got more and more real, spookily so. At first the tendency was to monsterize him. This process not too far from victimizing: fatness, spots, weakness of character (ie: shared fears perhaps), but gradually he became more human, got friends, became more a classmate, less a fifth former, more a person you had to deal with, live with, talk to, engage with. But still someone who caused real pain, terrorized his friends and enemies. And even more so someone who was in trouble himself, at home, in school, in groups. Someone whose bad side was winning out.

This Bully Circle, which appears in the back of the Writings section as *What to do with Michael Tucker*, is the only one I have a record of. It was recorded by the BBC as part of a Forty Minutes documentary called *Bullies*, broadcast on 30th November 1989. In fact, this was the first Bully Circle I did. The group was surprisingly uninhibited by the camera and sound-recordist, but in later circles I felt it was important for there not to be any distraction: the empty chair would be the focus, the people would 'talk and listen' to each other, not to a microphone.

At first the created bully (and it was discovered in doing this that groups do 'create' bullies) was a monster. Boys typically imagined a premature hulk, a bruiser with a mob, a big fat hideous misfit etc. Girls tended to make the bully two-faced, more of a manipulator than a lout. Both ascribed powers of influence and subjugation of almost mythical proportions. Encouraged by their peers to fill the imaginative space with giants and witches, the participants came down with a bump when I reminded them that the bully was in their class.

Then, in talking about friends and status and social acceptability, the group cut the bully down to size. He or she became human again, just another second year, just someone with an image to keep up, and their own struggles.

This is the crucial stage of the exercise. You could call it the moment of empathy. It is also the moment when imagination touches base and offers a way forward rather than a way of escape. That is, in fact, what empathy is: 'listening' to another person and discovering you are 'listening' to yourself.

This was why, halfway through this first Bully Circle, I was able to heave my heart into my mouth and say:

Well we have got a problem haven't we? Are we going to leave it?

No, they said, in unison. And at that point I knew all my work had been worthwhile.

And I knew we could go on to the next stage, which was talking about the bully as if each of them *was* the bully. They suggested reasons for the violent behaviour, the enslavement of friends, the persecution of certain victims; they confirmed the consensus rejecting bullying behaviour as anti-social (to be outcast, expelled and punished); and they offered advice on how to change it (by warning, befriending and getting help). And all the time they were doing this they were talking about themselves. If they had done the 'work', they had found out their own capacity for bullying behaviour, and so they knew what they were talking about. This is why the talk was now so serious.

Underneath ran a sub-text of unspoken but shared discovery. It went: If I am cruel to someone , I want my cruelty rejected. I cannot live with it. I want it to be noticed, felt, abhorred and annihilated. But I don't want to be shut out myself, not expelled, not left without friends. I want help from above and support from beside me. I want, desperately, *not* to be a bully. Are you the same?

2: What are friends for?

The value and costs of friendship do not diminish as we grow older. In fact we grow to depend on our friends more as we depend less on those in authority over us. And so the workshops keep coming back to the question of friendship. In the Research Project we looked at the value friends have in being loyal, trustworthy, open, supportive, honest, wise and kind. We also considered the trust friends placed in us to be equally honest in telling them what we think, equally open about our feelings, equally ready to talk, listen and share.

And we acknowledged that friends have some influence over us — power even. But what do you do if a friend wants you to do something you think and feel to be wrong? Do you trust your own judgment and feelings, and risk offending or even losing your friend? Or do you do what you think will please your friend?

When there is a bully around, extra pressure is put on friendships. Most of the bullying that students know about goes on without the knowledge of the teachers. It is their problem, their secret, often a guilty secret. Because most bullying does not affect the smooth running of the school, the teachers, who seem to be busy with important matters, don't always look into the 'little' problems children have with each other. Do you remember? Perhaps someone 'looked' at you, stared you down from across the classroom. Perhaps a new nickname was invented to make you feel small. Perhaps your old mates did not let you play with them any more. Perhaps you were teased. These are 'little' things, childish things even. But to a child, other children pose *life-size* problems.

If a person being bullied is lucky they have a teacher who will take them seriously, a carer who will listen, counsel, and not just say: 'You'll grow out of it'. But even if they don't have someone adult to talk to, they still have friends.

In the Bully Circle, the group reflected on the power of friends to support those in need and to confront bullies. A bully, it was noted, was often someone without 'real' friends, only people too scared to stand up to them. Which was confirmed by my interview with one boy who had this to say about his friends:

A friend is someone who is always on your side. Who always sticks up for you.

What about if you are doing something you know is wrong. Do you still want your friend to agree with you? Or do you want your friend to say: 'Hey, that's wrong and you know it!'?

It depends what the thing is. I think a friend shouldn't be like a slave, who does whatever you do. But sometimes I feel, yeah, I like somebody to do something for me. That's alright.

Do you have any friends who are slaves?
(laughs) Yeah, some of them.
What do you think of them?
Not slaves, but they usually do what I want them to do.

In the case of Michael Tucker, the group soon decided that one of his main problems was with his 'friends'.

His friends are scared of him. They are just his friends so that they won't get beaten up. He thinks he wouldn't have friends if he wasn't hard. He thinks we would think that he was a wimp and wouldn't play with him.

At first they proposed to withdraw their friendship from him, to punish him for his bullying behaviour, but in the end the consensus was to use it to try and help him:

If a few of us just started being good friends to him, and maybe show him that all of us do sometimes have the same problems as him, maybe he might think of us as good friends, and stop bullying.

3: Imagination and Fantasy

The Bully Circle began as an exercise in imagination. It required a degree of concentration and willingness to share which was not always there. At the school I talked about at the end of the Second Workshop, I arranged the circle for the start of the third workshop and opened the exercise in my usual way. Several candidates were proposed for the empty chair, some of them real third-year girls, but the group had great difficulty settling on an imaginary figure. The main problem was that they were not used to listening to each other, even though they were quite prepared to listen to me.

The talk needed to focus on a specific person so that everyone could make their own specific contribution, but it kept slipping off and being privatised between neighbours. And the less it dealt with the objective (but imaginary) figure of the bully, the more it became subjective and general: 'I'm not afraid of anything', 'I can beat up bullies' etc. In this case the opposite of imagination is not reality but fantasy: a personal fantasy image. And as a result the circle talk became much less of a shared experience. I soon realised how much talking I was doing, and how little serious 'listening' was going on.

So I stopped. I reckoned that if we went on to discuss 'dealing with the bully' with this shortage of consensus, it would only confirm some of the boys' fantastic self-images. I didn't think it would do much good having these fantasies aired ('Teachers don't care', 'Beat up bullies', 'Kill them' etc) and going unchallenged except by me. Several students pointed out that some of the teachers were themselves aggressive; I had already noted the class's low self-discipline and tendency towards macho gender roles. One of the few things agreed in our circle-talk was that children at this school did not think it was a good idea to tell their teachers about bullying.

When I came to do this exercise in another mixed school, this time with a third-year class, one boy also consistently introduced personal fantasy elements opposed to the consensus. While others shared their experiences of bullies and offered possible reasons for their behaviour, this boy wouldn't relinquish his dream of one-to-one combat. As I noted in my diary:

> The girls led the way in humanising the demon that the boys were pitting themselves against. But X, and some of the others, whether they knew they were doing so or not, sabotaged the gradual realisation of the bully-charac-ter, by interjecting macho fantasy elements. It is a smart defence, and an adult one too: the use of fantasy as a barrier.

And particularly ironic in this case since the consensus bully is big and fearsome, whereas the actual wielder of power in the class is small and smart. Is it always the case that teenage girls can perceive in psychological terms what boys have difficulty in releasing from the physical? Boys do objectify their fears and desires on to body parts (own, other people's, women's). They will see fighting as the kill or cure-all.

And the same boy had a problem with *imagined reality versus unreal fantasy* in a subsequent role-play. He was playing the teacher receiving advice on what to do about a bully whose parents he is just about to meet:

The Teacher

What shall I do?
You can't lie to them.
I'm going to have a headache tablet.
Look you can't lie to them. You have to tell the truth.
Don't listen to her...
The only thing I'm worried about is either him killing me or I'm killing him.
He's going to try to get you out of the school. You might lose your job.
I've heard Victor Duncan does weights. Is that true?
You should start weights then, and kill him.
Tell the truth. The truth is more important.
I heard he picked up thirteen dumb-bells.

Even without the video from which this was transcribed, you can see how he led the others away from their roles and into his dominant fantasy. From research in the previous workshop we had found out that this boy, though smaller than average, wielded quite a lot of power in the class: '... the weird thing is he doesn't really have that much power over kids shorter than him; it's the ones that are taller than him that he has power over. It's really funny.'

It is not that fantasy is not important and powerful. Most of the workshops were centred on the children's own experiences in school and at home, but I could not forget that many of a child's important experiences are imaginary. Made-up. Fantastic. And as such they often get disregarded by adults whose view of what constitutes real life can be amazingly narrow.

I remember dreams and stories from when I was six years old, but can't recall one 'real life' event that happened to me that year. I remember the fantasies I used to spin and doodle in history lessons far better than the history itself. And as for the effect of books and comics and TV heroes on my early formation, who knows?

It seemed important in the workshops to make some connections between the classroom, the *inner* fantasy life of dreams, day-dreams, nightmares and the *outer* fantasy life of stories, films, songs. Especially since the first few years of secondary school seem to be when both an enormous quantity of fantasy is consumed, and a lot rejected as childish. It is also the age when children begin to realise that fantasy can be a way of escaping from problems rather than solving them. With this might come the discovery that 'imagination' finds new ways to something, while 'fantasy' offers an old way to avoid it.

And so in a few of the workshops I decided to set writing tasks which deliberately tapped the area of personal fantasy. I could have done the same in dramatised ways but I wanted to keep the acting more or less an imaginative reconstruction of the children's own lives. Fantasy writing has well-understood conventions, whereas I find the form too unstructured for 'useful' drama.

Story-telling

AIMS:　to explore solutions to bullying (in a magic fantasy)
　　　　to suggest its origins (in a fantasy nightmare)

Magic

Your long-lost uncle has brought you a present from the South Seas.

It is magic anti-bullying potion.

This is good because there is someone in your year at school who is becoming more and more of a bully.

What do you do?

Illness

You are a popular member of class.

You look smart, you are a bit cheeky towards the teachers, you have an elder sister/brother who keeps you up to date with fashion, gossip & jokes. You have your own gang of friends.

Then things go wrong.

You get ill and miss a whole term of school.

What happens when you go back?

One example of the Illness story is in the Writings Section (p104). Here is a Magic story:

The Magic Anti-Bullying Potion

It was four o'clock in the morning when the postman came and delivered a parcel to the door.

It was for me. I ran up to my room and locked the door behind me. There was a card with the parcel. Who could it be from?

I read the card slowly, and when I got to the end I couldn't believe it. It was from my uncle. I hadn't heard from him for five years.

I dropped the card and quickly tucked into the parcel. There was a little jar with green, mouldy liquid inside, and a little label saying:

  ANTI-BULLYING POTION.

I burst out laughing. How outrageous could my uncle be? I had never heard of such a stupid thing.

But then it hit me. Michael Tucker! He had been such a pain for so long. Could this be the answer to my prayers?

The next morning I jumped out of bed and rammed my breakfast down my throat. Then I got a glass of water and poured some of the green liquid into the glass. It all dissolved quite quickly. I then plucked up the courage to drink it.

'Yuk' It tasted like a piece of garlic that had just been thrown up by a dog.

All of a sudden I felt stronger, and my voice sounded deeper. I ran out of my house and jumped on the Number 26 bus. In fifteen minutes I arrived at school. There was a big crowd of people in the middle of the playground. I raced over to see what was happening.

In the middle of the circle was Michael Tucker. He was having a fight with Billy Brown. I couldn't stand it. Michael was killing him. I pushed my way to the front and said:

'Hey, you. Leave him alone!'

But then Michael came after me. We got into a fight. Everyone was clapping their hands and cheering, especially when Michael fell to the ground...

Inside me I felt the ANTI-BULLYING POTION wearing off. I saw the teacher striding out from the staff room. I was safe. The bully was caught. But would my teacher believe me if I told her the truth?

In fact the last paragraph was written by me, as the two boys who had made up the rest couldn't think how to end the story before the bell went. And this points up one of the problems of fantasy: where does it end? Of course that is its delight as well: a self-generating urge, a flight from limitations, a constant picking up, dusting down and starting all over again. And fantasy can be a source of energy and renewed belief in our own capacities: if I am capable of imagining myself doing this or that, then the possibility of doing them can seem more real. On the other hand, if in my fantasy I give myself too much power and cool togetherness, then I can lose touch with what I really think I might do.

In an exercise called *Positive Thinking*, I tried to offer a way of grounding a personal fantasy in a 'real' self image.

Positive Thinking

NB: encourage pupils to look beyond their school selves
      can be used as a questionnaire or exercise

AIMS: to promote awareness of personal uniqueness
       to balance the pupil's self-image

Think about yourself.
Think about the things you can do.
You can think, laugh, speak, jump, cry. Lots of simple things.
You can do difficult things too.

1) Write down 2 or 3 things you can do which everybody here can do.
2) Now write down 2 or 3 things only some of the others here can do.
3) Now write down 2 or 3 things no-one here can do except you.
4) And 2 or 3 things you can't do yet but wish you could.
5) To finish with, use these ideas to write a speech about yourself. You could begin with your name — like this...

    My name is Francis
    I can swim but maybe you can too
    I can sign my name with an f that looks like a j
    I can..

This was another exercise that I had tried in the early stages, but found worked better later on. It also had given me qualms since it didn't seem fair on deaf children, although the problem, I now think, lies more in language-perception than anything else. 'I can' seems at first to refer to physical abilities and skills, or broadens in the school context to include academic achievements. But we also use the word in ways which are not physical, not academic: 'I can put my little brother to bed', 'I can understand why you are angry', 'I can stay up to watch the fireworks'. And I found the exercise was more stimulating when preceded by some of this language work. By the way, 'can' and 'know' come from the same ancient root.

The Writings Section contains a sample of answers to the first three questions. To the 'fantasy' question, number four, asking for three things they couldn't do but wished they could, many answered: fly.

At first sight this may seem the ultimate in escapist fantasy, not at all balancing in terms of a child's self-image. Though flying, of course, would be a spectacular way of avoiding bullies. Wouldn't an exercise like this in fact encourage children to fantasize their way out of a situation, rather than facing up to their responsibilities? I don't know. But I remember as a child I had dreams of flying too — mostly down staircases, as it happens.

Experience has taught me that no real flight lives up to the dreams of it. And that the dreams of it are not about physical flight at all. If anything they are about release, letting go, floating free, soaring, seeing oneself from above, or just plain getting away from it all. And these are all things which it is more possible, though by no means easy, to achieve than personal physical levitation. And often they are positive feelings confirming our autonomy, balance and freedom. But are they a result of the fantasy, or is the fantasy a result of them? What are the uses of enchantment?

3: The Third Workshop

a) Ethics

What I found, about one month after beginning the workshops, was that what I was doing was not, as I had originally thought, writing, drama and a sort of therapy, but sessions on ethics. By ethics I mean an exploration of right and wrong conduct in terms of how it links individual feelings of good and bad with shared hopes for a just society. The key question is: What is accepted behaviour? And it is one to which children are constantly giving ethical responses: That's not fair. That's well out of order. Why should I?

Eventually I wanted to promote an understanding of bullying through empathy with the bully's own situation. But first we had to deal with fear. It's all very well considering the bully's violent behaviour as a symptom of oppression and self-hatred, but unhelpful to expect a victim to see it as an expression of psychic crisis. In the short term violence brings the goods: power, status, money. If children are being bullied, they are so awed by the apparent superiority of the bully they find it impossible to stand up to them. If they had been able to cope they would have done; now, they can't. They need help. And they need help from their classmates as much as from an adult.

One of the ways that bullies get power over other children is by seeming to be more 'strong'. They have channelled their resources into their strong, fearless side, and split off the weak, frightened side until it is blocked from view. Thus they appear very powerful. The others fear them. Their fear confirms the bully's self-image. But it also reminds them of their own fear which they have hidden (fear which often comes from having been bullied themselves). And so they displace their oppression on to someone else.

When bullying is going on, however, it is not just the bullies and the people they are picking on who are in difficulties. Everybody who knows faces a dilemma: Am I involved in this? Do I get involved? Do I seek advice? Do I tell a teacher? Because what's happening can't be switched off like the television, it impinges too much on the life of the class. You can pretend it isn't there, in the same way as you can pretend you don't have feelings of vulnerability, but this very act of blocking becomes your involvement.

There is an adage: Doing nothing supports the oppressors. It is the same in a class where bullies rule. But 'doing nothing' is in fact an active process of repressing what you do not want to know. If a pupil sees a weaker member of the class humiliated by a bully and decides it is none of their business, they are blocking out knowledge of their own 'weak' side, and trying to get by with their 'strong' side alone. But this is just what the bully has done. They are now allies. When Becky speaks out about Eugene's bullying, she tells Sam: 'If you aren't willing to help, you may as well have hit him yourselves.'

In the workshops the group can do 'work' to practice dealing with the specific ethical problems posed by bullies. If the group have practised making up their own mind on difficult questions, they won't be so easily led by those who appear to be strong. If they have practised asserting themselves with the full weight of their judgment and feelings when they know something to be right, then they won't be cowed by insults. If they have practised taking responsibility for all their feelings (including 'negative' ones), that is, if they have 'got it together', their bravery will show up the bully's's bravado.

I wanted to find an exercise which would practice the making of difficult ethical decisions without ignoring 'negative' feelings. From my own experience I knew that I share a tendency to shy away from these. Life would be far simpler if we didn't sometimes feel scared, hateful, vulnerable, or worthless. But we all do. When we talk about extreme situations we often pretend we wouldn't be affected by these emotions: 'I wouldn't be scared', 'I would remain calm', 'I would phone the police immediately'. But when it comes to it, we find that banishing fear was the work of a coward, and our bravery is routed from within.

I needed to find a safe way for the members of the workshop to admit and acknowledge the reality of 'negative' feelings. Only then could they balance them against their 'positive' feelings, and build on both to decide what to do and how to behave. There is no bravery without fear. In the *Dilemma* role-plays which follow, I found a way in which they could help each other to dramatise the struggle that goes on inside them.

As usual I approached the main exercise through a linked series of warm-ups and technical 'rehearsals'. The idea of this was that by the time the game focused narrowly on bullying, the actors would have begun to emerge from 'engagement' with the technicalities of the game into 'expression' of their own full contribution. I stated in advance that part of the workshop would be filmed on video, and I let this give a shape to the following warm-ups:

Butterflies

NB: a joky, energetic prelude to film or stage work

AIMS: to loosen up

         to acknowledge and tackle stage fright

Form a circle.

The group leader explains the game by saying:

Do the opposite of what I say.

I am a Famous Film Director. You are going to be filmed.

Don't be nervous.

(Everybody acts nervous. Including the Famous Film Director!)

Hey, relax everybody.

(Everybody gets tense)

Don't worry — you won't be able to act if you worry.

(Everybody looks frightfully worried)

Don't cry...

(Everybody etc)

Be brave...

Come on now, you mustn't be frightened...

Embarrassed? I'm not embarrassed...

Stop giggling...

Don't laugh...

Look I said don't laugh...

Now quit screaming will ya? (This must, of course, be screamed) etc... ad lib.

Variations: get someone else to lead; get everybody miming an action at the same time — like making up or putting on a costume; with deaf children cut out the framing device if it seems too complicated.

The advantage of the game format — in the tradition of O'Grady Says — is that concentration is enhanced but not at the expense of having a good time. Besides, doing the opposite of what they're told to do comes naturally to most twelve-year-olds. But there is a deeper level to the game, which doesn't have to be picked up on here: in real life what people do is often the opposite of what they say. And when it comes to expressing feelings, it is very common for the tongue to betray the heart. Those who insist they are not afraid probably need to.

I didn't think it was necessary to dwell on this game, trusting that if it worked as a warm-up, the deeper level would look after itself. I reckon that one exercise can either feed into another or be fed into by another; it is too much too ask it to do both, and I wanted these warm-ups to feed into the Dilemma exercise later. If I had switched now from engagement to reflection, and brought to consciousness the 'meaning' of the game, it would not have fed into what was to come so much as swamped it.

The next warm-up followed straight on from Butterflies and maintained the film-set atmosphere:

Mirror, Mirror

NB: needs even numbers (leader can join in)
   encourage cross-gender pairs!
AIMS: disciplined fun, similar to 'moulding'
Get in pairs.
(Divide into 'A's and 'B's if necessary)
Face each other.
One of you is a mirror (A).
The other (B) is getting ready to be filmed.
It is your big break and you want to look your best.
Mirrors mirror!
Swap around and repeat until everyone is beautiful.

Variations: polishing the mirror; trying to catch the mirror out (a la Marx brothers); distorting mirror.

There may be a few technical hitches at first, with confusion over movements being mirrored or parallelled; and there might be some hyperactive or reluctant mirrors. Boys I've found more likely to be aggressive towards their mirror-image, girl pairs generally find more to do, and cross-gender pairings cause all sorts of hullabaloo. Movements of brushing hair, applying make-up, and even picking noses can be achieved by most pairs with a bit of practice: it is rather like remote-control 'moulding' and has the same mixture of 'Do as you would be done by' with 'Do what you can get away with'. But the breaking point almost always comes with eye-contact.

Again it would be possible to stop and reflect on this: why eye-contact is threatening, the part it plays in face-to-face encounters with bullies etc. And in one school I did make this connection. But as before, and with time pressing, I decided to push on. Remember that these warm-ups, for all my lengthy explanations, only last a few minutes each.

Next I turned to the voice, and a routine suggested by Penny Casdagli. Needless to say, I didn't use this one with deaf students:

My Dad has got a head like a ping-pong ball

AIM: voice warm-up
Get in a circle.
Leader starts chant (possibly to the tune of William Tell):
My Dad has got a head like a ping-pong ball.
Very rhythmic, very slow, then faster.
Emphasise words, consonants, exaggerate lip movements.
Now divide into two groups.
One group continues with the chant, the other goes:
Ping-pong, ping-pong, ping-pong BALL.
Accelerate and finish on a grand flourish.

Variations: divide into more groups (eg: My Dad / My Dad has got a head / Like a ping / Like a ping-pong ball); mimic styles of singing (Madonna, opera); bob up and down in rhythm. Etc.

From this I moved immediately to another rhythmic voice exercise:

I made my baby brother cry

AIMS: to elicit spontaneous cruelty and kindness
Stay in circle.
Leader starts a rhythmic clap, and chants:
I made my baby brother cry... by jumping on his toes.
All repeat.
Leader explains the game (in time if possible):
You mustn't let the clapping stop.
Everybody has a go.
I made my baby brother cry... by stealing all his toys.
Indicates it is next person's turn. All say:
I made my baby brother cry. Next person adds:
By eating his banana.
All repeat.
And so it goes on. When it gets back to the leader it changes to:
I made my brother well again... by giving him a hug.
Etc.

Variations: it is possible to alternate the verses; 'sister' works equally well; pace can accelerate to keep the game brief.

It's a minor point, but worth noting in passing, that people playing this game are more inventive being cruel that they are being kind. All manner of ingenious tortures get blurted out, emanating — I hope — from the fantasy life rather than the planning department, but the kindness usually consists of either undoing the evil or offering a sweet. Of course I had the bullying situation in mind when I was setting this up, but I thought I'd produced a balanced game — though it's true I'd put the bad bit first. I chose the figure of a baby brother/sister to illustrate two points: one that people you are *aware* of being cruel or kind to, are usually younger/smaller/more vulnerable than yourself; and two, that they are often also *close* to you (so close sometimes that you cannot see yourself doing it). I hoped that by making the cruelty and (lack of) kindness more conscious, this exercise would also suggest how easy it is to be thoughtlessly cruel. But again, now was not the time to dwell on this.

What I was working towards was the Dilemma role-play, which I developed from an idea Gillian Emmett had passed on to me. To set this up I did the following rehearsal:

Dilemma

NB: best initially with 3 chairs, the middle one in front
            only really works with groups of three

AIMS: to prepare for Bully Dilemma
            to promote 'strong' decision-making

Leader explains:

A dilemma is when you can't make up your mind.

You are, in fact, *in two minds* about something.

In this drama game you must make a decision.

You have two Angels to advise you.

But the Angels disagree with each other.

They sit behind you, one at each shoulder.

They are the thoughts in your head.

Your *two minds*.

(Here the leader gets two volunteers, puts one in the 'hot seat' slightly in front of where they and the other volunteer sit. They are Angels advising a Human on their dilemma)

For example:

The Human is sitting alone at a table, licking its lips.

Human	Shall I eat this cream bun?
Angel A	Go on! You love them.
Angel B	But you've had two already, you greedy pig!

Human	Well, I think I might, but...
Angel A	If you don't eat it, your sister will.
Etc.	

After they have given their advice, the Human makes its decision.
And, if possible, acts it out.

Class divides into groups of three.
Leader explains that everybody will get a turn at each role.
Also that pupils should try to use their own dilemmas.
If this is too difficult, the following examples can be given out:

You are going out to a party. Do you wear what you want or what is in fashion?

Do you accept the sweet being offered to you by your enemy?

Do you phone your friend right now?

Do you tell your boy/girlfriend that you now like someone else?

Do you tell your teacher the *real* reason for missing school yesterday?

You can't do your science homework. Do you ask the cleverest student in the class for help?

Your friend has told you, in secret, that she is in trouble. You think she needs help. Do you tell your parents?

You are going to be punished for breaking a school window. You didn't do it. You know who did. What are you going to say?

The first place I tried this was a Catholic school and the pupils immediately identified the angels as God and the Devil, or temptation and conscience. This was understandable, and the reason I'd chosen to call the adversarial advisors Angels rather than, say, 'advisors' was that I wanted it to be clear the dilemma was an internal one, that the voices were inside the Human's head (and, yes, metaphysical). To this end I arranged the seating so that the Human did not face the Angels (avoiding that dreaded eye-contact), but sat between them facing forwards. The Angels were so close that they only needed to whisper in the Human's ear (unless they started interacting with each other, which often happened, most amusingly).

With sign language the Angels and Human had to face each other, which made the exercise more social and 'real life', but the psychological roles became much harder to maintain (and after initial confusion I decided it was better to play this as a friendship-group exercise).

For the rest, I was aware that the idea of Angels was common to most religions, but I didn't want to limit the roles at the outset to 'Good' and 'Bad' (or worse 'Evil'): the two voices could be brave/cowardly, weak/strong, active/passive, clever/foolish, daring/timid, as well as plain good/bad. The important consideration was that each person got both sides of their dilemma *expressed for them*. They were made aware of and forced to acknowledge 'negative' feelings along with the 'positive' ones, and had to make a decision on what to do in a specific situation which incorporated both. What is more, they were made to embody all the roles, realising that everybody has these two sides to them, perhaps even bullies.

Which is why I rapidly moved on to the next stage of the workshop called:

Bully Dilemmas

NB: some preparation helps (see above)
AIMS: to explore in full the dilemmas of all affected by bullies
        to practise difficult decision-making
        to promote peer counselling

1) Individual Dilemmas

Remain in 3's from previous exercise.

Leader gives out the following roles to the person in the 'hot seat':

You are a bully.
You approach the person you are bullying?
What are you thinking?

You are the person being bullied.
The bully is coming across the playground towards you.
What are you thinking?

You are a friend of the person being bullied.
You see the bully approaching your friend.
What are you thinking as you approach?

You are a friend of the bully.
You see your friend bullying and making someone cry.
What are you thinking?

You are the teacher on duty in the playground.
You see something which looks like bullying.
What are you thinking as you approach?

It was at this point that I fulfilled my promise of filming the workshop. In one school I had taped this role-play, but found that the microphone (and my presence) had got in the way of the free flow of angelic conversation. It had also meant that the actors remained seated. With the video camera I was able to keep my distance, keep all three actors in view, record all that was said, record all the vital expressions and gestures, and even allow a certain amount of stand-up acting. In schools for deaf children, the video was even more essential in this and other exercises: it was the only means to record sign-language and preserve these role-plays for later reflection.

I found that when the actors remained seated, the Dilemma remained verbal, which encouraged the Angels to find subtle as well as impassioned arguments for their points of view. But if the actors were allowed to move around, a lot of the subtlety transferred to their body language and the verbal tussle became more repetitive. Some examples of these Bully Dilemmas are in the Writings Section (p105). It helped enormously if there was another adult in the room, as a lot was going on at once and the role of camera-operator involved shutting one eye.

I tried filming each Dilemma in turn, with everyone else watching, and this worked well with confident students but inhibited the less so. I tried filming each one in an adjoining room, which tended to make the Dilemmas longer and more intricate, but left the rest of the class impatiently waiting. I tried filming one group while other groups were rehearsing all around me, but this interfered with the sound-recording. In a school with deaf children, I filmed while Noel McDermott, my colleague and a fluent signer, played the role of Director. The best session of all was when the BBC filmed our workshop: it made everyone involved, including myself, feel very professional and accomplished.

Depending on how these role-plays went, and how much time was left, I then went on to put some of the ingredients together:

2) Meeting Dilemmas

NB: has to be preceded by some rehearsal of 1)
AIMS: as above, but introducing a social dynamic
Roles from the previous exercise meet.
(Avoid having bully and person bullied meeting — the conclusion is foregone.)
Two new roles are introduced:
Parent of the bully
Parent of the person bullied
Each has two angels, as above.
The meetings are tricky to arrange, but a teacher's desk or a dining-room table can help to shape the drama.

Options:
Teacher meets Parent of person bullied.
Teacher meets Parent of bully.
Bully meets Friend of person bullied.
Bully's Friend meets Friend of person bullied.
Person bullied meets Teacher.

Friend of person bullied meets Teacher.

Etc.

It's best just to do a few.

It *is* possible to do multiple meetings, for example between the Teacher, the Parent and the Bully, but the effect of having 9 people interacting is more surreal than edifying. Try it. Once.

These encounters are very difficult to record in any way. It is part and parcel of the exercise that everybody talks at once, and it becomes impossible to think straight amid the babble of voices. Isn't this what happens in a real-life crisis? Social relations are no less baffling — and even more complex — but they rarely go on with so much honest noise. In the circumstances, I was surprised at how many decisions were reached, and at the sheer ethical rightness of most of the decisions that were. In one school where the Bully Circle had shown no great enthusiasm for involving adults in dealing with bullies, the Individual Dilemmas almost all resulted in a much-agonised but resolute decision to confide in a teacher.

I wanted these Bully Dilemma role-plays to help the group *make up their own minds*. And as often happens with psychological processes like this, it was found that having people act out your mind for you made it easier for you to 'own' it. You own mind was no longer private property. Because when it is, and you are on your own, you are tempted to refuse to 'own' feelings and thoughts that you disapprove of: 'What me scared! You must be joking', 'Own up Francis', 'I wasn't myself — I never lose my temper'. And if you make up your mind in the sense of making-it-up-like-telling-a-lie rather than making-it-up-like-reconciling-two-people-who-have-had-an-argument, you will suffer the consequences. Or perhaps make other people suffer the consequences.

Because what was also, and crucially, going on during this exercise, underneath all the metaphysical paraphernalia, was — just as in the Bully Circle — a *counselling session among friends*.

Both during the acting and afterwards, when I replayed the video recording and we looked at the results, the whole group was sharing their problems and their fears. They opened their angelic/devilish hearts. They listened to each other, and as they did so they were listening to their own negative as well as positive feelings. They advised each other on the ethics of behaviour. And in the end each of them got a chance to make up their own mind fully and strongly. And it was all a game.

b) Close to the bone

Returning from a workshop in South London one afternoon, I was sitting on the top deck of a bus, at the back. The bus was full of children from the school I'd just been in, including one of 'my' students. I was clutching the Neti-Neti video-camera and reflecting on the successes and failures of the afternoon's session: we had done Dilemmas.

It was a while before I became aware of something happening at the front of the bus. A boy of eleven or twelve was provoking a girl of the same age for some reason. As he teased and prodded, and adopted a mock boxer stance, she tried to ignore him. Her 'friends', who filled all the seats around except the one next to her, did nothing. Suddenly she could bear it no longer, and rose to defend herself: and at the same moment, my neighbour and I intervened, she with her voice and me by evicting the boy from the bus — which he was probably getting off anyway. He wouldn't say his name, but he looked like a first year. A young bully in the making.

I felt terrible. Why hadn't I moved sooner to defuse the situation? Maybe a sharp, teacherly 'Oi' would have settled him earlier. And all the time — about 30 seconds or so — I half watched the teasing and harassment, I should have picked up on its real meaning. How often does pretend aggro turn into real pain-causing? I wondered if another reason I was so upset might have been because it was a boy bullying a girl. At a conscious level I'd approached bullying in a fairly impartial way: I knew that boys bullied more than girls, and with more physical violence; I also was reminded often enough that girls bullied, especially in psychological ways, although I'd seen one role-play where the boys were quite prepared to choreograph their attack, whereas some of the girls took the opportunity to kick for real. But now I was made aware of my deeper horror of male violence.

In adult life, the context in which we use the word 'bullying' is commonly one of a relationship. If adults are attacked in the street we call it mugging or assault. If adults are plagued with innuendo or abuse we call it harassment, but never bullying. However when the relationship is very close, at work or in the home, we often hear the phrase: Well, s/he's a bully. And when it comes to marital tension and the covert threat of male violence, bullying seems just the word to use. The fact that it is often used jokingly could — if we follow Freud — be indicative of the awe in which our childhood experience is held. Many adults still fear to tread in school buildings.

It is interesting in this context to note the history of the word''bully' and other meanings it still has for us today. A 'bully-off' in hockey is a fair contest between evenly matched opponents vying for the ball. 'Bully for you!' is a little used alternative for 'Good for you!' and has very positive connotations. Going back a bit, Shakespeare has 'bully Bottom' and 'Bully Doctor', with no hint that these are anything but chummy epithets. Dr Johnson gives us a clue with, 'The bully and the bawd who fatten on their misery', meaning that the bully is a pimp 'protecting' a prostitute. Is it surprising then that in the past 'bully' has been synonymous with 'lover', 'darling', 'gallant', and even 'mate' or 'brother'.

It is a word born in intimacy. Over the centuries 'bully' has moved from meaning loving partner, to boastful protector, to brutal exploiter. But this is not just a linguistic change. We are the living history of our language, and our words continue to describe us even when we don't know their origins. Relationships still degenerate from love to protection to exploitation, and the word 'bully' can still send a shiver of close fear down many a spine.

If in adult life then, we sometimes find bullying in a relationship, in childhood we find it *as* a relationship. The bully's actions are designed to bring about the closest possible daily contact: the victim is forced into an intimate relationship. I was often struck by the extra-ordinary intimacy of this bullying relationship. In one role-play illustrating the dilemma of whether to tell the teacher about a bullying incident, a group of boys enacted a playground bullying scene which we recorded on video. The smallest of the boys was the bully:

That's my bus fare!

Alright Martin?
John.
Chris.
Lend me twenty pence.
I haven't got any money.
Jump up and down. (He does so and jingles.) What's that then?
I don't know. Empty out your pockets. What's this?
That's my bus fare.
Someone's going to be walking home tonight.
I can't get home.
I don't care. You shouldn't have lied to me. I might need to rearrange your face...

(Friend intervenes)
Keep out of it!
No!
Fifty pence tomorrow, right? (Exit)
Why don't you tell the teacher?
Because he'll beat me up, won't he?
No, he'll get suspended.
Yes, but his friends will beat us up.

Then they'll get suspended.
Yes, but the teachers are not going to believe me, are they?
Try it.

As this bully made his threats, he closed in almost delicately on the victim, who was much taller, and put his face right up close. His threats were soft-spoken, cool and intimate. He then turned to the victim's friend and warned him to keep out of it in the same way, pulling the boy towards him by the lapels. Face to face.

Perhaps there is cultural influence at work here. It is the classic pose of man-to-man menace: noses touching, the staring down, outfacing imposition of submissiveness. Using the power of the face isn't confined to boys playing at being men, but it already has that edge of sexual difference: male physical contact, even only eye-contact, tends to use intimacy to express power. Which can, and often does, lead to violence. In my diary I noted:

> The word *'feisty'* is a Jamaican dialect word now current usage in London schools. It means 'cheeky'. They pronounce it 'facety'.

> It suggests thrusting your face in someone else's, brazening out a superiority — as in bare-faced cheek. It links with being cheeky, lippy, keeping your chin up, outfacing, facing up to, facing down etc.

> With the boys it seems to be a key reason for antagonism. Very challenging. Even threatening.

However the bullying starts, it becomes more dangerous the more it develops into a relationship. Like most relationships, once both parties know they are in it (willingly or not), it is increasingly difficult to get out of. Survivors of bullying speak of *years* spent trapped in this special hell. From the letters that Neti-Neti has received, we find examples of bullies whose attentions are similarly close up and intimate. One writer says:

> It is true when they say that your best friend can be your worst enemy. I fell out with my 'friends', and school life became hell. For nearly two years I was bullied. Not physically — they were cruel enough not even to allow me the pleasure of hitting back, but mentally.

Another remembers her second term at Primary School.

> The teacher asked me to be friends with, and look after a new girl. This child became my tormentor for three years. She pinched and kicked me, tore my clothes, controlled my activities and forced me to spoil my schoolwork.

I didn't think that my workshops had so far dealt closely enough with this aspect of bullying. One of the reasons that victims are reluctant to tell other people — teachers, friends, parents, even siblings — is that their victimisation seems so personal, so private. It is as if the bully's picking on them convinces the victim that there is something wrong with them, something so bad that they are ashamed to admit it.

I had tried to avoid using the word 'victim' in the workshops, even though it was a convenient shorthand and most secondary schoolchildren were capable of grasping its abstract meaning. 'Person being bullied' or 'Person being picked on' were not elegant substitutes, but at least they didn't imply the substantive existence of a being born to suffer. It was my firm contention, underlined by all the exercises I set up, that in the wrong circumstances anyone could get bullied.

But how to avoid it? I wanted to find a game which would practice persuasion, being persuaded and not being persuaded. If the strongest individual defence against a bully was not to let them persuade you that you deserved to be picked on, then everyone could do with some practice. I knew that Michele Elliott, the founder of Kidscape, had built assertiveness training into her excellent programmes with primary schoolchildren, but reckoned that just practising saying NO! to bullies in a loud voice might seem too simplistic with older pupils. In this exercise, I use buying and selling as the frame for work on resisting unwanted persuasion:

The Hard Sell

NB: can be used before role-plays or Dilemmas
          needs pen and paper
AIMS: to explore powers of persuasion
         to practise resisting unwanted persuasion

Everyone write down three things that you would never, never buy.

For example, things you hate, find disgusting, ugly, frightening. Eg: *orange lipstick, a Ford car, platform shoes.*

Now get in pairs and sit facing each other.

Swap pieces of paper.

Choose *one* of your partner's things.

You are a shopkeeper. Your partner is a customer.

Try to sell her the thing you have chosen.

Persuade her to buy it, talk her into it.

Now change roles and repeat the game.

   Did you persuade her to buy it? How?

   Did she refuse to buy? How?

If there is time, repeat the exercise with the other things.

Are you getting better at selling? Better at refusing to buy?

The above questions could be asked after the first round, or at the end of the game. This time, I reformed the circle and asked for reflection on the results of the exercise:

These were some of the ways found to persuade people:

1) *make it cheap and easy to buy.*
2) *try to understand why the customer doesn't like it.*
3) *make the customer feel the need to follow fashion.*
4) *make the customer feel guilty.*

And some of the ways to resist buying what you don't want.

1) *really know what you don't like*
2) *refuse to be drawn in to the game*
3) *trust your own judgment and feelings*

The relevance of this game to the theme of the workshops is not immediately apparent to the children, only becoming so as role-plays are introduced about persuasion. For instance in one situation a girl tries to persuade a friend into joining her in picking on someone they both don't like very much. This other girl has a difficult job resisting the proposal but the whole group can help in finding arguments to back her stand. The lessons learned in this exercise might also feed into the Dilemmas, and make the Angels more subtle in their advocacy. In that case, it could be brought to the group's attention that persuasion can be welcomed as well as resisted.

This game involved a non-threatening relationship which children understood and recognised as also part of the adult world. Indeed most of us at some time have been persuaded to buy things we don't really want, and we have also experienced the 'bullying' of those trying to sell us stuff. That we can use the word 'bullying' about insurance sellers, second hand car dealers and professionals peddling advice we don't accept, without it seeming out of context, also suggests the latent violence of the seller/buyer relationship. I call it:

The Trade-Off

Bullies don't steal from you, they make you buy them off. Stealing is merely the transfer of property, but bullying involves transfer of power. A thief snatches in the hope that the victim won't see, won't challenge, won't recognise. But the bully wants to be confronted:

Give me 20p.
No.
Give me 20p or else.
Or else what?

And the bully draws the victim into an exchange, a trade-off.

This is the start of a trading relationship. It is more openly based on the exchange of 'goods' for 'money' than most social relationships. But what does the bully sell? What does the victim buy?

The victim pays the 20p but is left with no tangible 'goods', and with the sinking feeling that, now trading has started, tomorrow the price will rise to 30p. But this is money given to the bully, not taken by him (let's make this hypothetical one male), and it feels like it must be in return for something, some service perhaps. Call it 'protection'. 20p's worth.

Protection is insurance issued by thieves. Even 'insurance' only buys a feeling of security, not security itself. But a money value placed on feeling secure makes the act of 'insurance' (or 'protection') into an understandable trade-exchange rather than a con-trick. From the victim's point of view, it is saving face to be trading rather than kowtowing; and the bully's self-image is enhanced by offering an insurance service rather than a clenched fist.

But what is the bully really selling? Underneath, it is *fear*. The 'customer' buys 20p's worth and takes the fear off his hands. The bully has an excess supply of fear (either more than most children, perhaps, or not dealt out in appropriate ways) and wants to sell it. At first, supply is high and demand is low. No-one comes forward to take some of the fear off him. It is cheap, even free. But then the bully finds a likely buyer, perhaps someone who already shows a collection of fears. That's a good sign: it is easier to sell fear to the already frightened.

And so the bully moves in and displays his wares. At first the trade is in looks, words, names, common assumptions. Often the seller and customer share a sex, a status, a desire to fit in, a longing for more power. Underneath the words, the real trade becomes apparent, the selling techniques more hostile. The bully insults, and by his insults shows what he is afraid of:

You are fat!	(I'm afraid of being fat)
You are ugly!	(I would reject myself if I were you)

To a girl:

You're a slag/tart/lesbian!	(What is my own sexual status?)

To a boy:

You're a wanker/poof/virgin!	(I fear my own sexuality)
You're a loser!	(I have been humiliated, now it's your turn)

The customer can refuse to 'buy' the insults (as in the colloquial usage: 'I won't buy that') by not taking them personally, by letting them slip through his fingers back into the seller's hands. Or he can accept them and take them to heart — in which case he is already acknowledging there is a price to pay. If the seller sees that the customer wants to 'buy' his fears (disguised as 'protection' from fear), he states a price. Sometimes the customer can negotiate, but more often he has to accept the price. And in the same way that a slap on the back clinches a businessman's contract, the deal is *struck*. More importantly, buyer and seller now find themselves in a commercial relationship which 'legitimises' their continued interaction.

But fears cannot be bought and sold. If I'm afraid of spiders, or my mother, or the dark, no amount of money is going to buy the fear off me. If you are afraid of the water, my paying you a fiver isn't going to make you swim. It is the same with all strong feelings: money can't buy you love, babe.

In the case of bully and victim, both are fooled by this illusion. The bully thinks he has sold off some of the fear that is making his life a misery, but finds his stock undiminished. The victim thinks he has bought off the bully and protected himself, but finds he is in an unequal trade where the price is boosted daily. And of course buying the bully's fear makes him *more* afraid, more open to new fear, less able to escape. The relationship is no longer commercial but proprietorial. Indeed former victims, writing to Neti-Neti after two Thames Help! programmes, speak of having been 'slaves':

I have had many experiences of being the victim of bullying at school.To name a few: being urinated upon, being forced to drink urine and being used as a slave to the extent that my life was not my own. I think I am still suffering the psychological effects...

Although I was actually bullied by only four girls, in one way I feared the rest just a much, for by being bullied I was at least being noticed whereas to everyone else I was invisible... These girls caused me great distress and made school the worst experience of my life.

Other letters tell the same story. There comes a point where bullying takes on a gravity which sinks you to the depths of your being. It touches the deepest humiliations of pornographic abuse. Doing the workshops for two and a half months became intensely disturbing. As I wrote in my diary:

How tired I'm feeling. The actors too are feeling it in the bones. The violence, the grinding raw emotion, the memories opening up forgotten horrors of childhood, seeing parallels in adult life. Yesterday's workshop was the work of a tired man. Without myself trusting my convictions, could I expect individual pupils, let alone a whole class to respond likewise? And without it there is only a depressing, defeatist reflex against a violent world.

Pat Lister, an Educational Therapist closely connected with Neti-Neti, had asked me a while back about how I protected myself against the stress of this sort of work. I don't know if I do. If I don't take it on, and just go through the motions, it doesn't connect, doesn't affect, doesn't work. Is this what the actors feel too?

Because bullying is of its essence very, very threatening. Thinking about it, working on it, watching a gripping drama, all got to me. To such an extent that in the last week of the tour my nights were wrecked by a recurring dream, which I couldn't remember afterwards. It was a dream about connections, in which each link in the chain came out sparking from a furnace. The first time it came it was terrifying, the next time worrying, but the last time it seemed to offer a way through and I never had it again.

The strain affected me in another way too, in that after half a dozen viewings I could no longer bear to watch two scenes in *Only Playing, Miss*: where Eugene erupts in hate before Mrs Richards, and where Mrs Richards brings her divine fury down on Cheesy and Rant.

There was a change in her lines so that in performance Mrs Richards said: 'I'm not going to have you terrorise our other students in the school because you're enjoying being cruel' whereas in the original she'd said 'getting off on being cruel'. And I always 'heard' this version with its strong sexual charge.

With the children too, both as participants in a workshop and as the audience of a play, the subject matter got too close for comfort. There were tears, there was some highly defensive 'displacement ', there were meaningful silences. What I tried in the workshops was to be as non-threatening as possible, I didn't wish my work to contribute to fear but to reduce it. All the exercises were an attempt to get into the situation before the violence did, *before* the threat of violence or even before the idea of violence. There is very little understanding to be won from the sight of one person beating up another. Every punch is a closing down of options, every kick damages the chances of communication, every threat is an infliction of silence.

It is no good just role-playing an assault and asking children to discuss the problem of bullying. Yes, bullying happens like this in our playground. Yes, it should be stopped. There is nothing to discuss. The first casualty of bullying is communication.

4: Conclusions

'Behaviour'

No-one is born a bully. No-one is born to be bullied. Bullying behaviour is learned from others in real life. And real life is not good at showing children where they have gone wrong: by the time it does, it is often too late to learn from the mistakes.

But behaviour is a much misunderstood idea. Parents say:

I want you to be on your best behaviour now.

And we normally think of behaviour as something put on, something children do for other people, especially those with high status. When we hear:

She is well-behaved in class,

we make the assumption that the child is well-behaved towards the teacher. Perhaps we extend this to include the other pupils, but the two sorts of behaviour do not always go together. In talking with children about who is likely to bully, I found many examples of angels to the teacher being devils to the other children. This was called being 'two-faced' and was considered a highly undesirable characteristic.

What we often do *not* mean by 'behaviour' is that the child is well-behaved in herself. There isn't really a word for it, but the nearest is the slang expression 'together'. Someone who has 'got it together' is *well-behaved,* in that her behaviour is not dependent on who she is with. She will carry herself with the same composure whether she is with her irritable aunt or obstreperous friends. Similarly, she realises that the worst sort of *misbehaviour* is when she does something that is at odds with herself, not merely inappropriate.

When we say: *Behave yourself!* we are (rightly) imposing our social criteria of behaviour. We mean: What you are doing doesn't conform with standards of behaviour we consider appropriate in this context.

We lose sight of the meaning: *Be yourself!* But this is what behaving means. Behave. Have our being. Carry our being out into the world:

'Without crafte nothynge is well behavyd' Skelton (1526).

179

Which could be loosely translated as:

You won't get it together without practice.

But practice at behaving ourselves, being ourselves, is what we don't often get. We are too busy doing it for real. And when we make mistakes in behaviour, as all of us do, the consequences can be so frightening we would rather not be ourselves at all. It is a feature of fantasy, which is our comfort when we would rather not be ourselves, that the central character is incredibly well-behaved. Cool and collected. Together. Totally at ease with their own being. Or at least playing the part to perfection.

And this, of course, is where acting and imaginative fiction come in. They provide a space to try out different behaviour. Doing the workshop offers a variety of roles to experiment with safely. It gives participants a chance to learn how to be themselves by temporarily being other people. It is a chance to make the important distinction between 'behaviour' and being/feeling. We show that behaviour is not just 'good behaviour' shown to adults and teachers, but the whole range of how we behave to other people, our friends, enemies, ourselves.

We discover how we cannot really change who we are or how we feel, but we can, if we want to, change the way we behave. Also that people - both friends and parents — can disapprove of how we behave without losing their respect for who we are and how we feel. In turn, if we are set this good example, we can extend it into our dealings with bullies: rejecting their anti-social behaviour but accepting them as people. Of course, *acting* is the prime example of changing our behaviour but staying the same person underneath. In play then, just as in the first few years of our life we learned playfully, we can practise real life with the assurance that it is only pretending.

With this in mind, it becomes possible to explore the true gravity of bullying in a safe way. One of the final tasks of the workshops was a writing exercise called 'Problem Page'. The group had already done 'Dilemmas' and was now ready to imagine themselves into a role, and write a letter from it.

Problem Page

NB: a writing task in the last workshop
        individual or pair work
AIMS: to identify with all roles in bullying situation
        to work towards solutions

Problem Page 1

You have told your parents that you are being bullied at school. You are too scared to tell the teacher who is doing it. Now you write to the Problem Page of a magazine. Tell them your story and ask for advice.

Problem Page 2

You know what is happening in your class. One of your friends is picking on someone, just for a laugh. But that someone is getting hurt, and has even started missing school. Write to the Problem Page telling them about the difficult choices you face.

Letter to Parents

You are the Head of Lower School. You are writing to the parents of a student who has been discovered bullying other pupils and taking money from them. What do you say?

Letter to the School

You are the parents of a child who is frightened of going to school. Your child is being bullied, but won't say who is doing it. You have already spoken to the teacher. Now you are writing to the Head of Lower School.

There are some examples of these letters in the Writings Section (p107), but here is one more:

Dear Deirdre,

I am really upset and thinking of committing suicide. I am in the first year of secondary school, and have been bullied since the day I started the school. I don't think I'm that ugly, but I wear glasses and I am a bit overweight. I get called things like 'goggles', 'four eyes' and 'fatty'. I can't cope.

If I'm on my own, they trap me in a corner and start beating me up and spitting and throwing chewing gum at me. But the worst thing is that they are so good in class, and around teachers they deny beating me up, and I get in trouble for lying.

It's really getting me down. The worst thing about it is that they live around my way, and when I pass them to go to my flats they hit me. I've told my Mum, as I don't live with my Dad, but she is too scared to say anything as they have ruffian parents. I am scared for my Mum as she has trouble getting out of the flats because she gets abuse. On one occasion she got beaten up really badly because she complained to their parents, who were drunk at the time. Please help as I am desperate.

Consensus

The letters written in the above exercise were mostly individual efforts, although some students worked in pairs. To finish the workshop, I wanted something which would bring together the group as a whole so that the lessons each person had learned could be shared and, most importantly, so that the group could become aware of its new consensus against bullying.

Advice for New Pupils

NB: first in small groups, then together

        this is for real — the results should be published

AIMS: summing up lessons learned in workshops

        reinforcing consensus against bullying

Your group has been chosen to write a page in the booklet for new pupils called:

How to deal with bullies.

Think carefully of all the things you can do to avoid being bullied yourself, and to stop others being bullied.

Write them down.

Put the most important things at the top of the list.

Now show your list to the other groups. Compare them.

Try to agree on one new list.

Write it down.

This is your agreement.

Your contribution to the school's anti-bullying policy.

Display or publish the results.

For an example of this exercise see the Writings Section (p111).

Reaching a consensus is not easy. There is always the temptation to 'follow my leader'. There is also the temptation to follow the teacher, whose style of teaching, 'listening' and 'talking' contributes enormously to the ethos of the class. To teach someone is to lead them into a new area of experience, whether the experience is knowledge, understanding or behaviour, and this is not always done by teachers. Children are especially good at teaching each other how to 'behave'. And in teaching each other they themselves become empowered.

The problem is that some bullies acquire the status of leaders. 'That'll teach you!' they say, as they give someone a 'lesson'. They make their victims keep quiet, pay attention, speak when they are spoken to, not answer back, take their punishment ('like a man').

Of course, there is often leadership without bullying. Children may follow strength of character, looks, brains, glamour, skill or whatever. This 'follow my leader' may seem unsatisfactory from an adult point of view, but we probably all do the same. It is natural to want power and to want to use power: to give and receive praise, to be able to tell someone what to do, to feel needed, to have expertise, to be referred to, to be valued and respected. It is also a natural failing to misuse this power: children make mistakes in how they deal with people, as do adults, but with appropriate support (and luck) they will learn from these mistakes.

What happens with a bully is that they abuse another child in order to get power. Their behaviour pushes beyond accepted limits, and breaks a bond. This is very disturbing. There is no such thing as a small breech of an ethical agreement. Out of order is out of order. The bully becomes powerful because in making one breech they summarily replace consent with force. And force appears to have no limits.

If the bully can get away with this particular act of cruelty, then it is well on the way to becoming 'acceptable'. It is the now dominant bully who leads the way with new dares, forfeits, challenges, attitudes, extremes. Every time they 'succeed' in bullying someone — that is the victim accedes to the bullying and the group does not ostracise the bully — the new behaviour becomes available to the group. The ethics have changed, the group accepts this new area of experience, the lesson has been learned.

In adult terms, this is what happens when army recruits are 'initiated' by being made to witness, or even participate in acts of torture. The inhibition against causing pain and killing is strong, but army trainers do not need psychologists to tell them that peer group pressure can be stronger.

Peer group pressure can work the other way though (especially when there is no threat of court-martial). In the famous Milgram experiment (*Obedience and Authority*, 1974), two-thirds of one group of student participants in an 'experiment' proved individually willing to administer electric shocks as an aid to a fellow student's learning; but three-quarters of the other group defied the authority of the experimenter, once two 'colleagues' had done likewise. (The colleagues were planted and in both case the electric shocks were fake.)

This sort of peer pressure can be used against bullies: ostracism, followed by re-integration on the group's terms is an effective strategy. And very empowering for the group to win back the initiative. If bullying behaviour can be checked, the whole group benefits from a sense of ethical justness, and all the individuals are made aware of their own contributions. The link has been made between feeling good inside and doing the right thing in the group, where before it was a source of conflict.

In the final scene of *Only Playing, Miss* the group does just this: Becky and Jo lead the way in challenging Rant's bullying, and their brave ethical stand becomes available to other members of the group, such as Hashi and Cheesy. Rant is isolated, their fear of him is dispelled, and the process of understanding can begin. Becky, Jo and Hashi are brave enough to tell Mrs Richards about Rant's bullying of Eugene without 'understanding' the reasons for Rant's behaviour. But for Eugene himself, it was only when Mrs Richards had arranged a meeting between the parents, and he had understood Rant's own bereavement, that he was able to emerge from his own fear and silence.

Similarly in the workshops, the final reflection of the group is towards action *and* understanding. I feel strongly that they belong together. Without understanding bullying and why it happens, any action the group takes is likely to be ineffective, or even counter-productive: without action (as detailed in the Advice exercise), any understanding of bullying is likely to add to their sense of powerlessness. For example, part of the understanding of a bully might be that they have problems at home:

> *I think he bullies because of how he is treated at home, and just to get respect from all the younger children. He does it to get friends.*

But if this insight was made without a context of practical agreement, it could be quite daunting: the bully's home life and problems are completely outside the influence of the rest of the class. An obvious reaction would be: So what if his father beats him up, what can I do about it? Or: So, he's taking his problems out on his mates, what do you expect?

Only if there is a practical consensus to tell the teacher about bullying can this understanding be acted upon.

> *I think it is the teachers' problem. Just because he's outside of school they could still talk to him. They can help him with his problems. They could ask him to tell them what's going on at home. The teachers can do more about it than he can.*

And it is as a result of this acknowledgement of the necessary role of the teacher in sorting out a bullying problem that the class can act upon their own sense of responsibility. They have understood that bullying behaviour is ethically unacceptable and should be rejected whenever it occurs. They have understood that the bully suffers from a lack of respect and is trying to force it where it can only be given. They have understood that bullies have a big problem making and keeping friends. All these aspects of understanding can be translated into pupil action, but only if there is sufficient consensus in the class and a basic empathy with the bully as a person in need of help, rather than a monster.

If we gave him some help, like making him monitor for the books or chairs, and give him a role with power, give him something to do... he will get better and adapt and have friends, good friends.

Empathy, ethics, consensus. These were the watchwords of the workshops, and the process that I hope the workshops set in motion. The more I did, the more convinced I grew that the consensus had to stretch beyond the classroom walls and into the whole school. On its Autumn 1989 tour, *Only Playing, Miss* played to first and second years, but many schools who saw it wanted it to be shown to third and fourth years as well. It was appreciated that the play, and the workshops in the schools which had them, could contribute to an approach which embraced the whole school.

One of my main aims in conducting the workshop programme was to gather writings from the pupils involved, and a small selection of these is presented in the Workshop Writings on page 97 ff. But schools which take up the ideas in this book, or who see *Only Playing, Miss*, will have different aims.

They may want the issue of bullying to be more prominent in Personal and Social Education. They may want the English and Drama Departments to organize writing projects for display in the corridors and performances to be shown in assembly. They may want to work towards incorporating anti-bullying initiatives into individual class behaviour contracts. They may want to develop a co-ordinated whole-school policy which emphasizes the common responsibility of all members of staff and all pupils to create an ethos in which bullying behaviour is unacceptable. These are all aims which I whole-heartedly support, and I hope that this book will prove a useful resource for schools which pursue them.

RESPONSES TO THE PLAY

The Questionnaire

The Neti-Neti Theatre Company has always tried to 'listen' to its audience. To do this we need to provide a chance to respond to the play after, as well as during the performance. This is why we produced a programme booklet, containing the playscript of *Only Playing, Miss* and a selection of writings from the Workshops, and sold it to schools at a heavily subsidised price.

We didn't put on this play for 'the public', but for specific constituencies of young people. With *Only Playing, Miss,* as with our other productions, we wanted to make sure we were getting through especially to the deaf children, Bengali-speakers and second-language speakers in our audience. This was also our reason for doing the workshops. And we wanted to check if the play was reaching to the eleven-to-fourteen age-group we had asked to play to. (It was aimed at first and second years, but many schools wanted the play back to be shown to older classes as well.)

For these reasons we prepared two questionnaires for schools, one for the teachers and one for the pupils. The questions for the teacher were simply:-

1) *How did you, as a teacher, respond to Only Playing, Miss?*
2) *Did you feel that the play was interesting for your pupils?*
3) *Did the audience include any: deaf or partially-hearing pupils? Bengali-speakers? others for whom English is a 2nd language? What were their specific responses?*
4) *Did you encounter any practical difficulties in having the company perform at your school?*
5) *Do you think the play is useful as an approach to the problem of bullying in schools?*
6) *And the programme booklet?*
7) *Do you have any further comments or suggestions?*

On the back of the teachers' questionnaire I printed one for pupils, which I suggested could be photocopied or used as a basis for class discussion. I had intended this for use in the schools themselves, expecting that teachers might summarise their class response and send us the results. In the event, many schools chose to send us dozens of individually completed questionnaires, for which we are very grateful. Here are the questions:

Please answer these questions about our play. There are no 'right' answers. Try to give reasons for your answers.

Only Playing, Miss *is set in a school where most of the characters are pupils.*

They are called: Hashi, Jo, Sam, Becky, Cheesy, Rant and Eugene.

1) *Which of them did you like best? Why?*
   And least?
2) *Jo is Eugene's friend, Hashi is Becky's friend, Cheesy is Rant's. Which of the characters would you like as your friend?*
   Why?
3) *Rant calls Jo and Eugene 'losers'. Do you think anyone in the play is a 'loser'? Who?*
4) *Did your feelings change as the play went on?*
   How did you feel about Rant?
   About Eugene?
   About Sam?
5) *How has the death of a parent affected people in the play?*
6) *Do you think Rant is a typical bully, or an unusual one?*
7) *Are the girls in the play nicer with each other than the boys?*
8) *Jo advised Eugene to tell an adult that he was being bullied. Becky and Hashi told Mrs Richards.*
   What would you have done?
9) *Do you think that our play was true to life?*
   Which of the scenes or characters do you 'recognise'?
10) *Do you think that your school should do more to prevent bullying? If so, what?*

It was found that some of the questions had to be phrased more simply with younger deaf students, but that overall they covered most of the issues pupils were eager to talk about after seeing the play. It is impossible to give more than a brief selection of the responses. The reception of the play was very enthusiastic, and pupils (especially in schools with partially-hearing units) welcomed the use of Sign Language and Bengali. Reactions to individual characters and to dramatic incidents in the play were very strong, but mixed. As were assessments of bullying in the pupils' own schools: one would say there was no bullying, while another in the same class would say there was lots.

The play moved many of the audience to recall their own experience of being bullied or witnessing bullying. It prompted some very sensitive enquiries into what makes someone bully, rousing condemnations of such behaviour, and much real sympathy and understanding. These comments are taken from answers to the first nine questions:

Rant has lost the meaning of his life.

He is typical. Most bullies bully the person most like them: they hate themselves so they take it out on a similar person.

Rant is too wrapped up in himself to think about anyone else and care for them. It's the persons inner feelings that make them a bully.

Rant is a coward bullying to hide his feelings.

On the whole I thought the girls hurt Eugene more than the boys. Bruises and knocks wear off but words are never completely forgotten.

Eugene should have told a teacher earlier and shouldn't have kept his feelings about his dad dying bottled up.

I was frightened by Sam's funny, clever, cruel power.

Sam became almost compassionless. She just used her friends.

The death has made them so sad they don't want to communicate with anyone else.

There are a lot of people like Sam. She follows the boys but leads the girls.

He just wanted Eugene to feel the same way as he did when his mother died. Sort of like revenge.

He suffered the same thing as Eugene. And he knew what it was like. On the outside it was just all a front, but on the inside he knew what he was going through.

The part I enjoyed was when Eugene was talking to his teacher and he got into a huff and let out all the hate he'd stored inside him.

Sam is a loser because she lost her friends and was two-faced.

I would like Sam to be my friend so I could change her ways.

It made one person take out his sorrow on someone who is not as good at hiding his pain as he is.

The girls can talk with each other more than the boys.

Only losers could tease someone who had lost someone.

The girls pretended that Becky was not there, and that in a way is much worse than any physical punishment.

Sam's little game got out of hand.

My feelings changed from excitement to horror to sadness. I was horrified at the amount of times Eugene was beaten.

I liked Becky best. She was understanding, different from everybody else, and never leaves you out.

I liked Jo the best because all the way through he sticks up for his mate. He also gives very good advice and helps people. He was kind to Eugene, but not really unfriendly to anyone. He was there when Eugene really needed someone. Didn't hurt anyone's feelings.

And a comment from an older student:

In the end he actually started communicating with the bully, and standing up for himself. It was the teacher getting the parents together made him understand that Rant had problems as well. And so he felt that he wasn't alone. The play wasn't just saying go to a teacher and she will sort it out, it was also to do with communicating, and standing up for yourself personally, not just getting people to solve your problems.

And here are some of the replies to the last question about how schools can do more to prevent bullying:

Teachers should be more friendly so pupils feel at ease telling them their problems.

It's up to the parents to help prevent their child from bullying!

Bullying is always happening in one way or another.

I think my school tries ever so hard to stop bullying and succeeds sometimes. But if they are not told, how can they stop it?

Expel everyone that is caught bullying more than once.

Schools should have more activities at break.

Pupils should have someone to talk to if they need help

Keep the bullies in so they don't get to someone else.

I would have told as soon as it started. I have experienced it and it is the best thing to do.

Our school is a good community and we help each other.

Punish bullies well, but try to find out the problem behind it first.

Try and make the bullies understand they should not do it.

I have been bullied. I went and told the Dinner Ladies (by this time I was crying). The stupid Dinner Ladies just said: 'They're only playing.'

People who do bully others who have seen the play will hopefully think again before hitting someone.

Bullying is a major problem and people could do more to prevent it if they tried harder.

Bullies always lose if you really want them to.

The audience didn't chose to go to see the play. Maybe there were bullies in the audience who wouldn't want to go to this play.

Half my class are bullies, Miss.

This is not an excuse for bullying, but I feel that the bullies need help. This was a strong point that I felt.

Our school has shown us plays and made it clear to us.

I myself have been bullied and it feels like the end of the world.

Chase High School

response by Judith Mcgregor

It is notoriously difficult to assess attitude, but what we all hope has happened at the Chase High School as a result of Neti-Neti's visit with *'Only Playing Miss'* is a continuing change of attitude. 'We' in this case, are the teachers involved with both the deaf and hearing children, and 'change of attitude' implies a deepening awareness of the implications of both deafness and bullying.

Almost all the first-year pupils in the school saw the play, and all the hearing-impaired pupils, although most of them are older. There were also some deaf children from other schools and their teachers, including one teacher who is profoundly deaf and who teaches some of us signing.

I work as a support teacher within the mainstream English department, and so have many opportunities for incidental discussion with children.

The pupils at the Chase are fairly familiar with signing in their school, and some of them attend sign language classes run by the teacher in charge of the unit. Even so, there may be the thought that signing is something slightly mysterious, executed on the sidelines.

Suddenly, in the situation of the play, signing was seen not just a 'a' language, but as THE language — a real and powerful language, used by skilled people. Many of the hearing children realised the emotional force of sign language used as a dramatic medium. An important part of the play was seen as the fact that you could not avoid knowing what the actors meant when they signed as well as spoke. One boy said to me afterwards, 'Gosh, it's really scary when they do that!'

My own response to the signing in the play was of admiration and envy. How had these people managed to achieve such skill and fluency in a few weeks when I had been struggling away for a couple of years? Not only could they sign in the play, but they could also carry their skills into conversation with the children.

The hearing-impaired children were confused over who was deaf and who was not. Everyone realised that 'Becky' was deaf, but most though that 'Mrs

Richards' was not, even though her hearing aid was visible, and even though these deaf children know hearing impaired teachers.

It was a valuable experience for the deaf children to realise that other children could be victims too; that bullying and being bullied was not confined to those with hearing problems, and that verbal bullying could be even worse than the physical type. Although there are times in the classroom when we translate others' rudeness or foolishness, we are not there to interpret what goes on in the playground, and consequently our pupils may well be unaware of the extent of verbal nastiness.

As a group, the hearing-impaired children were riveted by the performance. Some of the signing may have been rather fast for them, and the slower children may have felt overwhelmed at one or two points.

However, the essential messages and emotional impact were fully conveyed. The only real confusion arose with 'Eugene's' song, 'There's a fire in my chest'. One older deaf boy took this to imply that 'Eugene' was going to set fire to the school, and asked a couple of times when the fire was starting.

A deaf girl with very limited language thought there was rather a lot of fuss about the boys' behaviour. This decidedly feminist pupil thought that boys were inevitably aggressive and stupid, and should just be ignored. She also felt that 'Eugene' was stupid to get so upset, and wrong not to be aggressive in turn. In short, it was not worth making a fuss about boys!

Another deaf pupil also felt that 'Mrs Richards' was in the wrong for both getting very angry and sending the boys to the headmaster. She should have done one or other, but not both.

'Becky' was unanimously liked by the deaf children because she was deaf, and 'Jo' because he was kind, helpful, supportive, reliable. 'Eugene' was generally thought to be understandable, although he might have done more to help himself; but Sam was regarded with horror. The deaf children used works like 'cruel' 'frightening', 'rude' (with its many other implications in deaf terminology), and implied that Sam's worst attribute was unpredictability — you just could not tell what she would do next, or, even worse, whether she was your friend or not.

The Chase High School has had deaf pupils for two years now, but this was the first time that sign language was seen to be used in a public performance by professionals, and this fact must surely enhance the status of others using it.

Hamilton Lodge School

Letter from Sara Head,
a deaf teacher of profoundly deaf students

Dear Penny,

Only Playing, Miss came to our school this afternoon — *brilliant*. It is an outstanding play — quite the best I have ever seen anywhere.

The script seemed perfectly aimed at *everyone* in our 11-17 age-range. No mean feat. And it had all the staff totally enthralled as well.

I took my class of profoundly deaf 9-11 year-olds, some with emotional and behavioural problems. They sat the whole way through, spell-bound. It was amazing to watch their faces when they recognized themselves in certain situations. It was so real — with so many situations we all identified with. You could have taken some of the phrases straight from the mouths of our staff and pupils! It certainly made them think.

The production was excellent and the standard of Sign phenomenal — especially as it was a mixed deaf/hearing cast. It was lovely for our children to be able to talk to the cast afterwards as well. There are not many theatre companies they can do that with.

One of my ten year-olds was very moved when Eugene was being bullied . I had to sit with my arm round him — he has been bullied. Actually there were times when I myself had a lump in my throat. I was bullied in my first year at secondary school — it brings back memories.

The morning after the performance, I discussed it with the children in my class. It had certainly made a big impact on them. They could remember everything that happened in the play. They wanted to act out some scenes. So we did.

We then talked the situation through and thought about how the characters must have felt. With the help of the blackboard, we considered what was acceptable and unacceptable behaviour. The children remained interested and involved in the discussion for a full hour and a half!

In the secondary school, the play gave rise to much classroom discussion about bullying and this culminated in a full-scale debate on how to deal with bullies, with the children as speakers, in a departmental assembly. Several also wrote essays.

Only Playing, Miss raised the profile of 'bullying' and identified it as being unacceptable to the peer groups in schools. Even now, many months later, my children still say to each other 'don't bully.'

Please write another play soon and don't forget to bring it to Hamilton Lodge!

SUGGESTIONS FOR FURTHER READING

Margaret Atwood, *Cat's Eye*, Bloomsbury 1989

Valerie Besag, *Bullies And Victims In Schools*, Open University Press, 1989

Michele Elliott, *Keeping Safe*, 3rd Edition New English Library, 1988

Michele Elliott, *The Willow Street Kids*, Piccolo, 1986

Elton Report, *Discipline In Schools*, HMSO 1989

Susan Griffin, *Pornography And Silence*, Women's Press 1982

Angela Grunsell, *Let's Talk About Bullying*, Aladdin Books, 1989

Gulbenkian Foundation, *Workshop On Bullying In Schools*, 1989

Alice Miller, *For Your Own Good*, Virago 1988

Mona O'Moore, *Council Of Europe Report On Bullying*, 1989

Delwyn P. Tattum and David A. Lane, *Bullying In Schools*, Trentham Books 1989

Delwyn Tattum and Graham Herbert, *Bullying: A Positive Response*, Cardiff, SGIHE,1990

Additional References

Arora C.M.J., and Thompson D.A. (1987) *Defining Bullying for a Secondary School*. Education and Child Psychology. 4.4 p.110-120

Askew S. (1988) *Aggressive behaviour in boys: to what extent is it institutionalised*. In Tattum D.P. and Lane D.A., (1988) *Bullying in Schools*. Trentham Books. Stoke on Trent.

Chazan M. (1988) *Bullying in the Infant School*. In Tattum and Lane op.cit. Dukes C. (1905) *Health at School*. Rivingtons. London

Herbert G (1988) *A whole curriculum approach to bullying*. In Tattum and Lane. op.cit.

Heinemann P.P., (1973) *Mobbing*. Glydendal. Oslo Lane. D.A. (1974) Truancy in the disruptive pupil. Conference paper ILEA London

Lane D.A. (1975) *Dependency:* techniques of prevention. Kings Fund/IEGC London

Lane D.A. (1978) *The Impossible Child* Vol. 1 & 2 ILEA London

Lane D.A. (1988) *Violent histories: bullying and criminality*. In Tattum and Lane op.cit.

Lane D.A. (1990) *The Impossible Child*. Trentham Books. Stoke on Trent.

Olweus D. (1978) *Aggression in the schools: bullies and whipping boys*.Hemisphere Press. Washington DC.

Orton W.T. (1982) *Mobbing*. Public Health.96.p172-174

Pikas A. (1989) *The Common Concern Method in the treatment of Mobbing*. In Roland E. and Munthe E. (1989) *Bullying and international perspective*. Fulton Books. London.

Reid. K. (1985) *Truancy and School Absenteeism*. Hodder and Stoughton. London

Reid K. (1988) *Bullying and persistent school absenteeism*. In Tattum and Lane op.cit.

Roland E. (1988) *Bullying the Scandanavian research tradition*. In Tattum and Lane op.cit.

Roland E. and Munthe E. (1989) *Bullying: an international perspective*. Fulton Books. London.

Sparks J.P. (1983) *Mobbing in an Independent Secondary Boarding School*. Public Health. 97.p316-319

Stephenson P. and Smith D. (1987) *Anatomy of the playground bully*.

Education 18th August 1987. p.236-237

Stephenson P. and Smith D. (1988) *Bullying in the Junior School*. In Tattum and Lane. op.cit.

Tattum. D.P. (1988) *Violence and Aggression in Schools*. In Tattum and Lane. op.cit.

Tattum D.P. and Lane D.A. (1988) *Bullying in Schools*. Trentham Books.

Titman. W. (1988) *Adult responses to childrens' fears*. In Tattum and Lane. op.cit.

INDEX OF EXERCISES
IN ORDER OF APPEARANCE

SECOND WORKSHOP

CONCLUSIONS

BY AIM